JUAN MARTÍN

Guitarra Solista

8 Concert FLAMENCO Compositions in MUSIC NOTATION for Classical Performers

INCLUDES:
Guernica
Alegría de Pablo
Farruca Martín
El deseo atrapado por la cola
Noche en los jardines de Granada
Con rumbo al Carnaval
El Tajo de Ronda
Taconeos

To access the online audio go to:
WWW.MELBAY.COM/30940MEB

WWW.MELBAY.COM

FLAMENCOvision
LONDON MÁLAGA

CONTENTS – CONTENIDO

Includes access to online audio of all tracks.
Incluye acceso al audio en línea de todas las pistas.
7 of the tracks available on all streaming services and on cd from flamencovision.com
7 de las pistas disponibles en todos los servicios de streaming y en compacto desde flamencovision.com
Videos available:
Search on YouTube: Juan Martín and name of piece.
Buscar en YouTube: Juan Martín y título de obra musical.
https://www.youtube.com/user/JuanMartinOFFICIAL
www.flamencovision.com

INTRODUCTION BY JUAN MARTÍN

These original compositions of mine have been transcribed in close supervision directly with me by Angela Centola, a fine classical and flamenco guitarist. She is a composer and concert guitarist who is part of a new generation of performers programming what they believe to be ideal repertoire in their concerts. Her knowledge of music notation has enabled me to put all technical detail of both hands onto the printed musical page and to bring to light these previously eight unpublished works in two separate volumes: this book in music notation for classical guitarists and others who read music and a separate volume of the same eight works for flamenco players in tablature/cifra.

Played in a recital, these compositions would provide enough variation in dynamics and tone colour for a full concert programme. Recordings of these works can be found on my albums *Guitar Maestro – the Juan Martín Collection, Solo* and *The Andalucian Suites*. There are also live concert performance videos of six of the eight compositions to be found on YouTube's JuanMartinOfficial channel and the online download URL to the recordings is provided in this book.

My website will also provide information on concert performances and masterclasses. My annual week-long course, 'El Arte Flamenco de la Guitarra', is held in Ronda, Andalusia, Spain in early July and anyone studying these pieces would be most welcome to attend.

Special thanks to Bill Bay for his support and encouragement throughout a long association.

Juan Martín.

INTRODUCCIÓN DE JUAN MARTÍN

Éstas composiciones originales mías han sido transcritas en estrecha supervisión directamente conmigo por Angela Centola, una excelente guitarrista clásica y flamenca. Es una compositora y guitarrista de concierto que forma parte de una nueva generación de artistas que programan lo que creen que es el repertorio ideal en sus conciertos. Su concimiento de la notación musical me ha permitido poner todos los detalles técnicos de ambas manos en la página musical impresa y sacar a la luz éstas ocho obras inéditas en dos volúmenes separados; éste libro en notación musical para guitarristas clásicos y otros que leen la música y un volumen separado de las mismas ocho obras en tablatura/cifra para flamencos.

Tocadas en un recital, éstas composiciones proporcionarían suficiente variación en la dinámica y el color del tono para un programa completo de conciertos. Las grabaciones de éstos trabajos se pueden encontrar en mis álbumes *Guitar Maestro – The Juan Martín Collection, Solo* y *The Andalucian Suites*. También hay videos de presentaciones en vivo de seis de las ocho composiciones que se encuentran en el canal de YouTube JuanMartinOfficial y el URL de descarga en línea a las grabaciones se proporciona en éste libro. Mi sitio web también proporcionará información sobre conciertos y clases magistrales. Mi curso anual de una semana de duración, “El Arte Flamenco de la Guitarra”, se lleva a cabo en Ronda, Andalucía, España a principios de julio, y cualquiera que estudie éstas piezas será bienvenido.

Mi agradecimiento especial a Bill Bay por su apoyo y estímulo durante una larga relación.

Juan Martín.

THE REPERTOIRE

GUERNICA (Tarantas)
This composition was inspired through Picasso's biographer, Sir Roland Penrose, inviting Juan Martín to perform at the 90th birthday celebrations of the artist. The bombing of the Basque town, Guernica, was portrayed in a short film made by Antony Penrose, Sir Roland's son, for which Juan composed the music (see YouTube). Following this it became a composition in three movements:

1. El Presentimiento (The Foreboding)
2. El Bombardeo (The Bombing)
3. El Lamento (The Lament)

ALEGRÍA DE PABLO
Composed to celebrate the birth of Juan Martín's first son, Pablo, this piece evokes the tender vulnerability of the newborn and the alegría (joy) of his father.

FARRUCA MARTÍN
The minor key farruca can be danced, sung or as in this case, presented as a solo composition. Played in 4/4 time it originates from the northern Spanish region of Galicia. A farruca can also allude to a woman from this area.

EL DESEO ATRAPADO POR LA COLA (Rumba)
This was the title of a short play written by Picasso, a copy of which was given to Juan. The title *Desire caught by the tail* is perhaps a metaphor for men as they grow older.

NOCHE EN LOS JARDINES DE GRANADA "Homage to Andres Segovia"
This composition is in the key of the granaínas and has several quotations from Manuel de Falla's orchestral work, *Nights in the gardens of Spain*. The *embrujo* or magical spell that pervades the Alhambra Generalife gardens at night was the inspiration for this composition.

CON RUMBO AL CARNAVAL (Guajiras)
Set in the guajiras rhythm, *On the way to the Carnival* is a joyous piece of music reflecting old Havana, Cuba's capital and the rhythmic vivacity of this island's people.

EL TAJO DE RONDA (Rondeña)
After the initial harmonics, the following arpeggio falseta evokes the sensation when looking down from the Puente Nuevo bridge into the abyss of the ravine, El Tajo. Juan Martín's guitar course, 'El Arte Flamenco de la Guitarra', is held annually in this dramatic mountain setting of Ronda, announced as La Ciudad Soñada – the dreamt city.

TACONEOS (Zapateado)
The zapateado was made well known by the Spanish violinist Sarasate and also by Antonio el bailarín (dancer), whose virtuosic footwork (zapateado) inspired the title of this solo, *Taconeos*; heeltaps.

EL REPERTORIO

GUERNICA (Tarantas)
Ésta composición fue inspirada por el biógrafo de Picasso, Sir Roland Penrose, quien invitó a Juan Martín a actuar en las celebraciones del 90 cumpleaños del artista. El bombardeo de la ciudad vasca, Guernica, fue retratado en un cortometraje realizado por Antony Penrose, el hijo de Sir Roland, al que Juan compuso la música (ver YouTube). Después de esto, se convirtió en una composición en tres movimientos:

1. El Presentimiento
2. El Bombardeo
3. El Lamento

ALEGRÍA DE PABLO
Compuesta para celebrar el nacimiento del primer hijo de Juan Martín, Pablo, ésta pieza evoca la tierna vulnerabilidad del recién nacido y la alegría de su padre.

FARRUCA MARTÍN
La Farruca, en tono menor, se puede bailar, cantar o, como en éste caso, presentarse como una composición solista. Tocado en tiempo de 4/4 se origina de la región norteña española, Galicia. Una farruca también puede aludir a una mujer de ésta parte.

EL DESEO ATRAPADO POR LA COLA (Rumba)
Éste fue el título de una obra corta escrita por Picasso, una copia de la cual fue entregada a Juan. El título, *El deseo atrapado por la cola,* es quizás una metáfora para los hombres y el envejecimiento.

NOCHE EN LOS JARDINES DE GRANADA "Homenaje a Andrés Segovia"
Ésta composición está en el tono de las granaínas y tiene varias citas de la obra orquestal de Manuel de Falla, *Noches en los jardines de España.* El embrujo o hechizo mágico que impregna los jardines de la Alhambra Generalife por la noche fue la inspiración para ésta composición.

CON RUMBO AL CARNAVAL (Guajira)
En el ritmo de las guajiras, éste palo es una alegre pieza de música que refleja la vieja Habana, capital de Cuba y la vivacidad rítmica de la gente de ésta isla tan musical.

EL TAJO DE RONDA (Rondeña)
Después de los armónicos iniciales, la siguiente falseta de arpegio evoca la sensación al mirar desde el Puente Nuevo hacia el abismo del barranco, El Tajo. El curso de guitarra de Juan Martín, "El Arte Flamenco de la Guitarra", se lleva a cabo anualmente en éste entorno montañoso espectacular de Ronda, anunciado como La Ciudad Soñada.

TACONEOS (Zapateado)
El zapateado fue conocido por el violinista español Sarasate y también por Antonio el bailarin, cuyo virtuoso zapateado inspiró el título de éste solo, Taconeos.

SYMBOLS AND NOTATION

Fingers of the right hand	**p** = thumb **i** = index **m** = middle **a** = ring **e** = little
Fingers of the left hand	① = index ② = middle ③ = ring ④ = little
>	Musical symbol to accentuate one or more notes
~	Vibrato, a sideways movement on the string, across the fingerboard
↑	A downstroke, from bass to treble
↓	An upstroke, from treble to bass
⌇	A wavy line before a chord indicates that it is played as an arpeggio from bass to treble
⌇ **p**	When the wavy line has an arrow and the letter **p** beneath it, it indicates that the arpeggio is played as a single stroke by the thumb from bass to treble
⌇	Arpeggio from treble to bass
↑ **ma**	A downstroke by the middle and ring fingers together, from bass to treble
↓ **ma**	An upstroke by the middle and ring fingers together, from treble to bass
i a m i	Trémolo
4	Left hand *apagado*. Sound damped by little finger across strings
R	Right hand *apagado*. Sound damped by open hand across strings
□	Golpe or tap, is produced with the middle and ring fingers together, or by ring finger alone, of the right hand on the tap-plate below the 1st string
⊗	Slap with three extended fingers (i,m,a) on the strings (from frets 15 to 19) and lower soundboard (high pitched sound)
G	Slap with three extended fingers (i,m,a) on the strings and lower soundboard between soundhole and bridge (low pitched sound)
O	Slap with three extended fingers (i,m,a) on the strings and lower soundboard over the right-hand side of the soundhole

SÍMBOLOS Y NOTACIÓN

Dedos mano derecha	**p** = pulgar **i** = índice **m** = medio **a** = anular **e** = meñique
Dedos mano izquierda	① = índice ② = medio ③ = anular ④ = meñique
>	Signo que se emplea musicalmente para acentuar una o más notas
~	Vibrato. Un movimiento de un lado al otro, a través del diapasón
↑	Un rasgueo hacia abajo, de los bordones hacia las tiples
↓	Un rasgueo hacia arriba, de las tiples hacia los bordones
⌇	Forma arpegiada de los bordones hacia las tiples
⌇ **p**	Cuando la línea ondulada tiene una flecha y la letra **p** debajo, indica un acorde arpegiado del pulgar hacia abajo, de los bordones hacia las tiples
⌇	Forma arpegiada de las tiples hacia los bordones
↑ **ma**	Los dedos medio y anular tocan juntos de los bordones hacia las tiples
↓ **ma**	Los dedos medio y anular tocan juntos de las tiples hacia los bordones
i a m i	Trémolo
4	Apagado mano izquierda – Sonido amortiguado por el dedo meñique (4) a través de las cuerdas
R	Apagado mano derecha – Sonido amortiguado por la mano abierta a través de las cuerdas
□	Golpe en la tapa inferior por los dedos medio y anular, o sólo por el dedo anular, de la mano derecha
⊗	Palmada de tres dedos extendidos (i,m,a,) encima de las cuerdas (desde trastes 15 a 19) y un poco de la tapa (tono más alto)
G	Palmada de tres dedos extendidos (i,m,a,) en las cuerdas y la tapa entre la boca y el puente (tono más profundo)
O	Palmada de tres dedos extendidos (i,m,a,) encima de las cuerdas y la tapa inferior al lado derecho de la boca

Guernica

Taranta

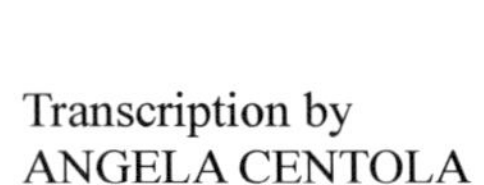
Transcription by
ANGELA CENTOLA

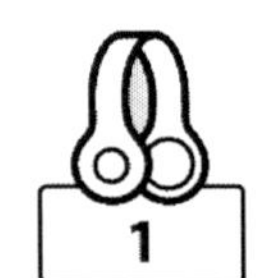

JUAN MARTÍN

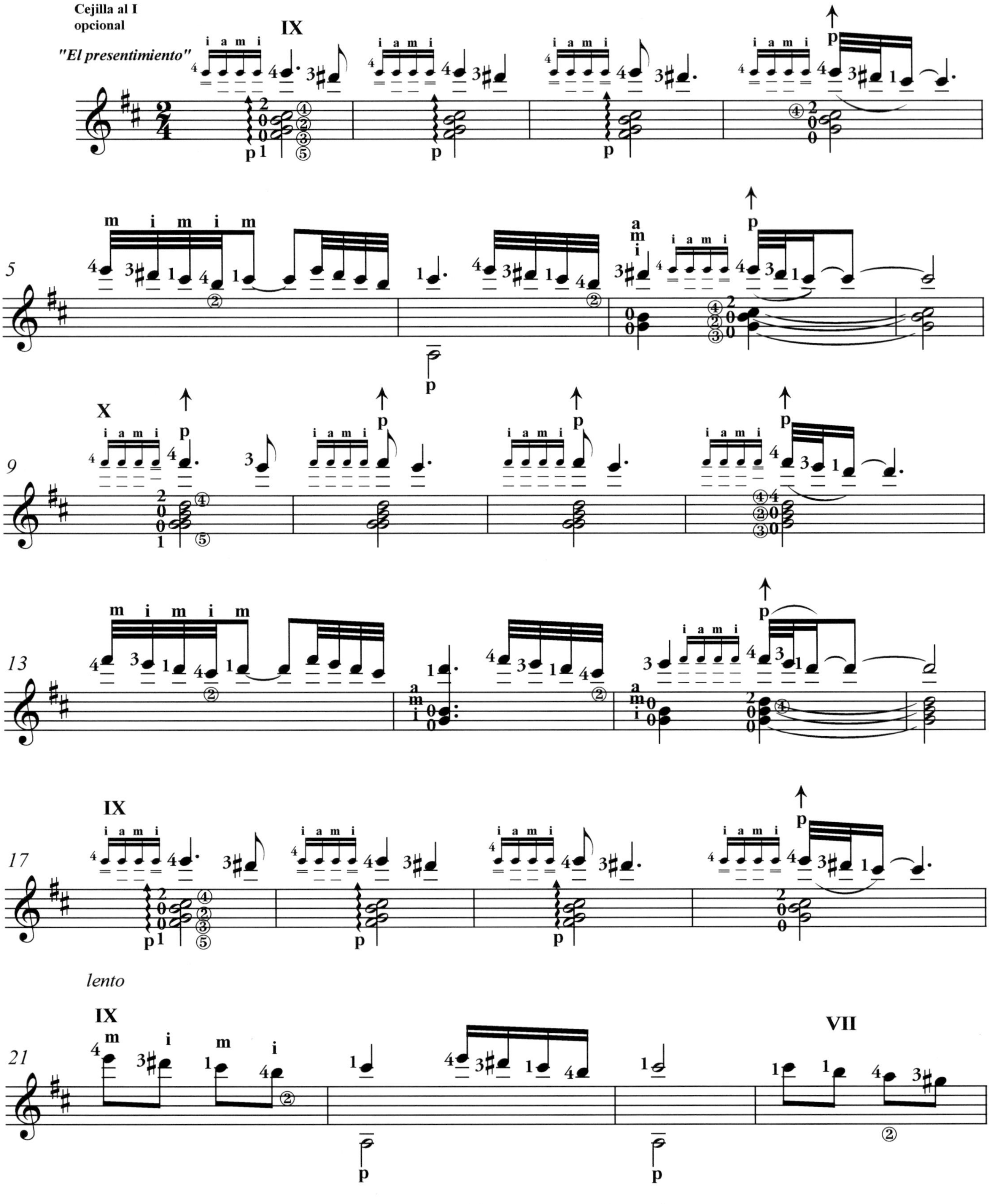

Cejilla al I opcional

"El presentimiento"

lento

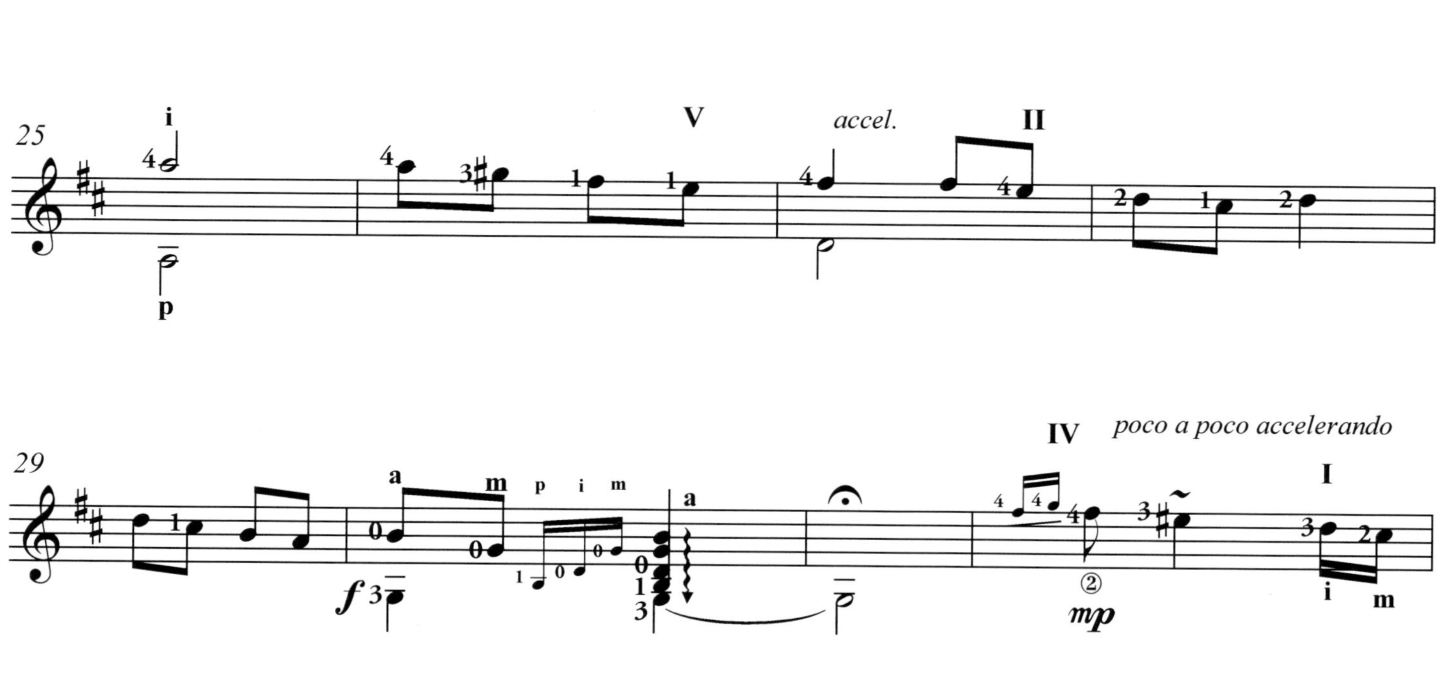
accel.
poco a poco accelerando

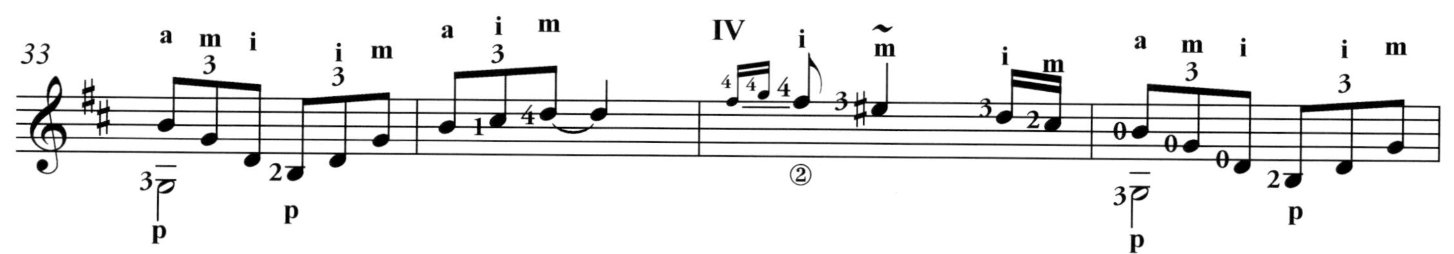

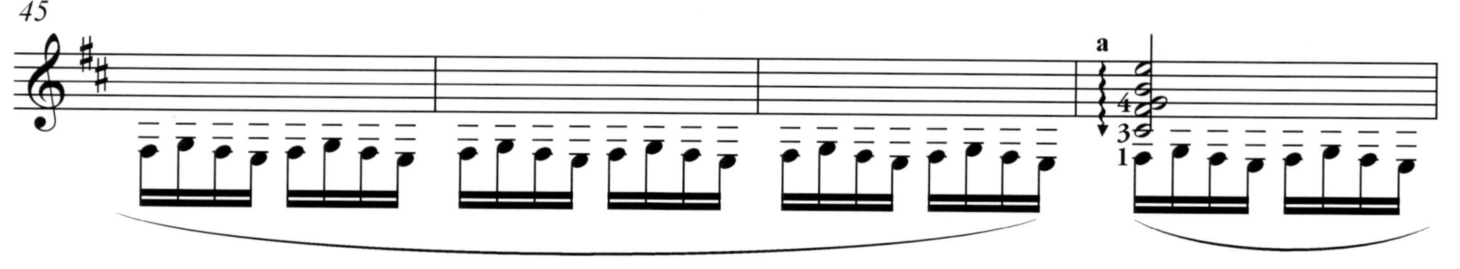

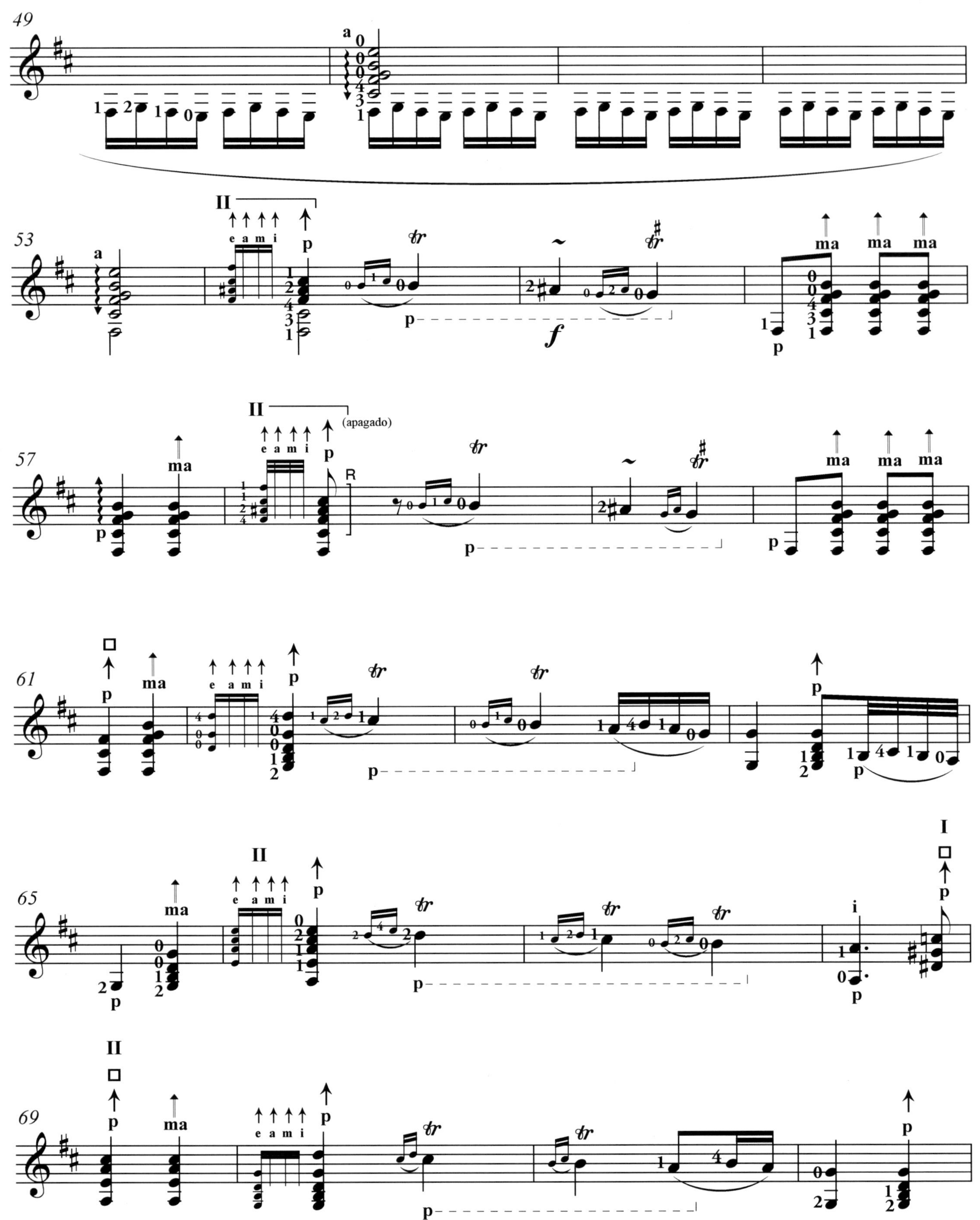

49
53
57
61
65
69
II
I
e a m i
ma
p
a
(apagado)
R
tr
f

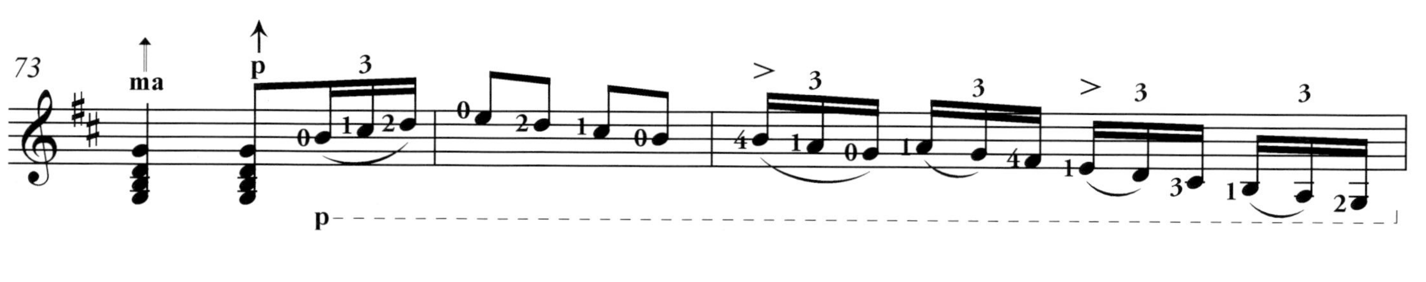
73
ma
p
p
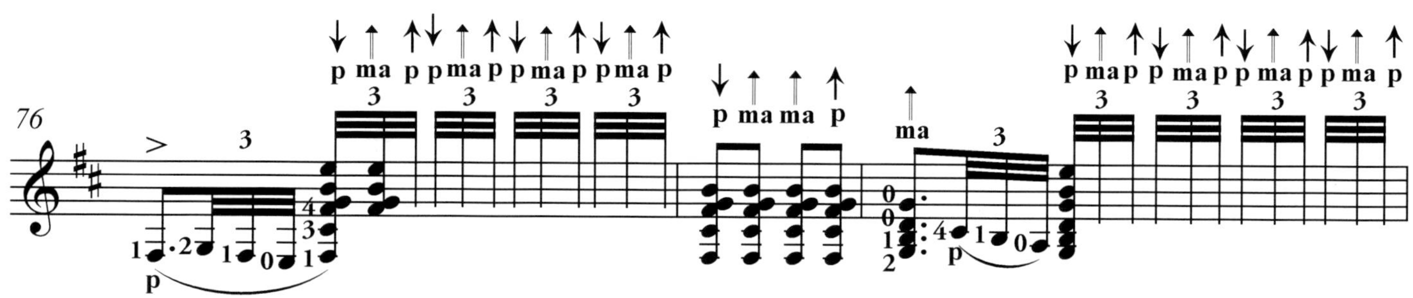
76
p ma p p ma p p ma p p ma p
p ma ma p
ma
p ma p p ma p p ma p p ma p

79
p ma p
ma
ma
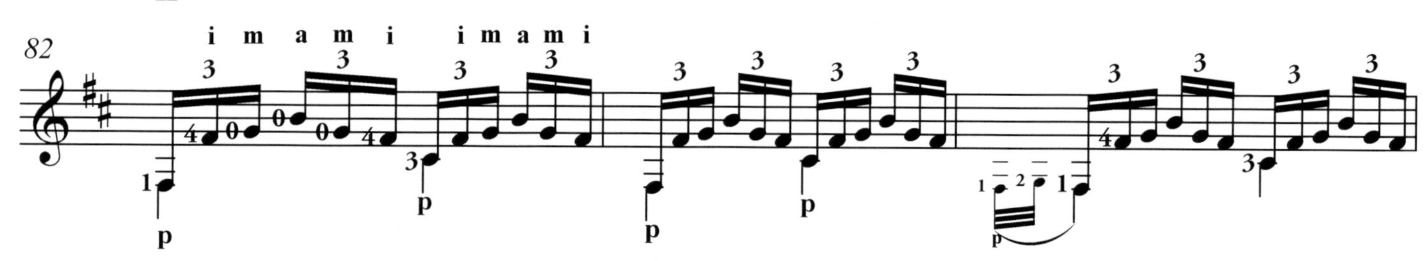
II
82
i m a m i i m a m i
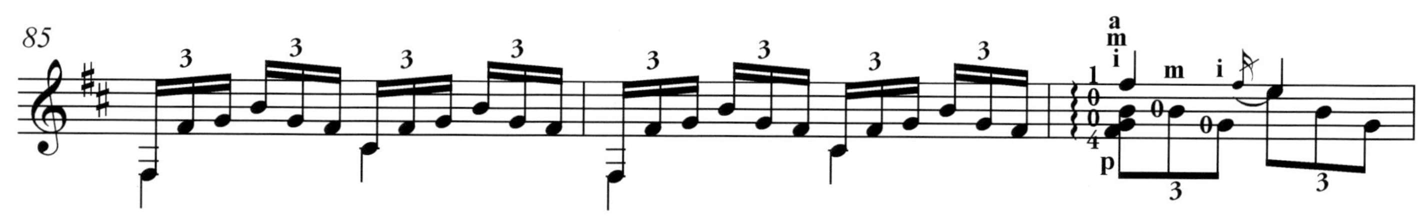
85
a
m
i
m i

88
i m a m i

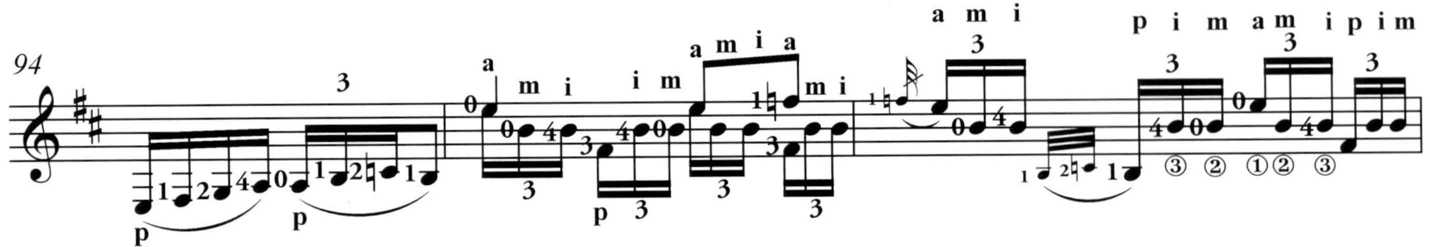

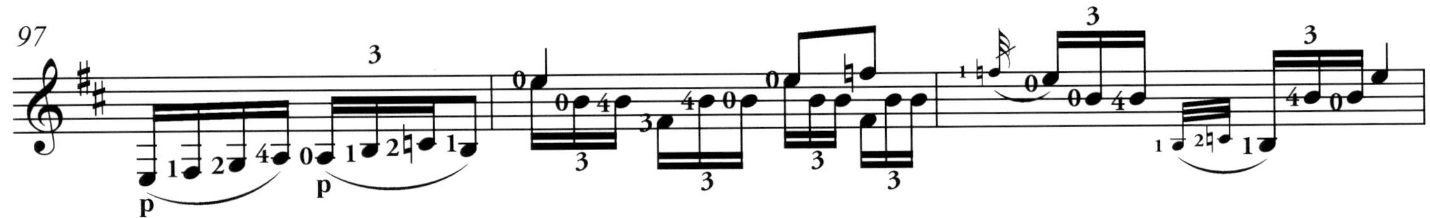

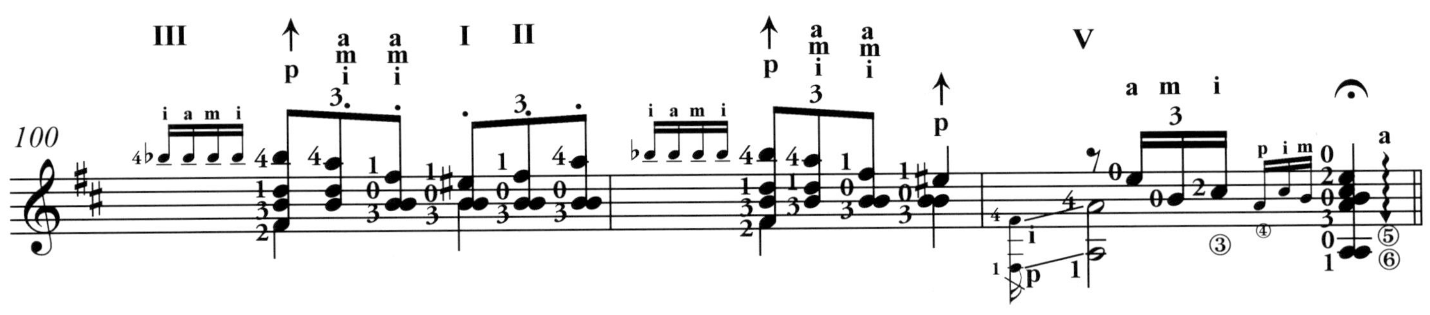

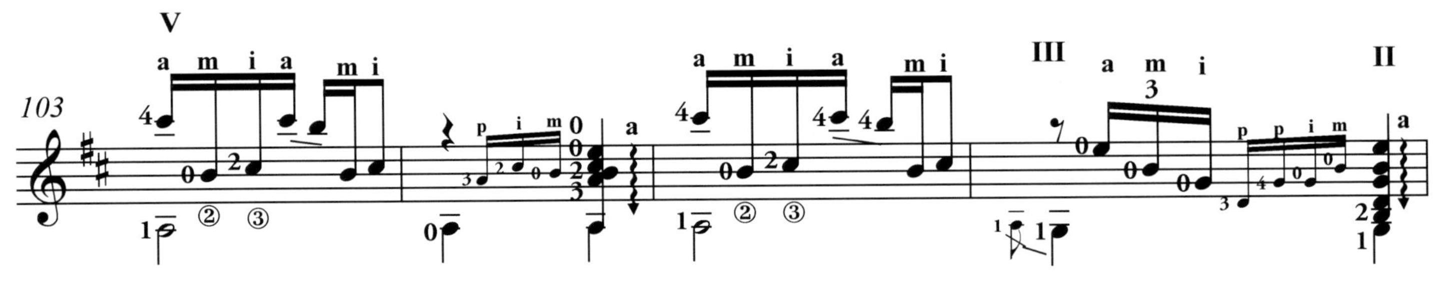

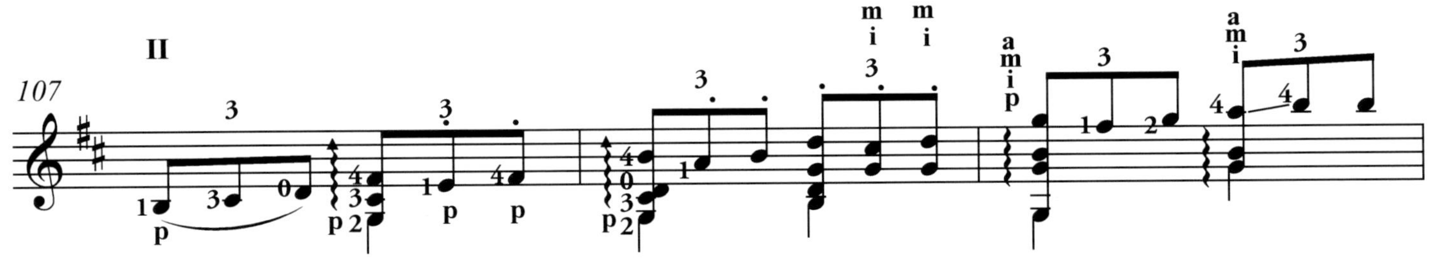

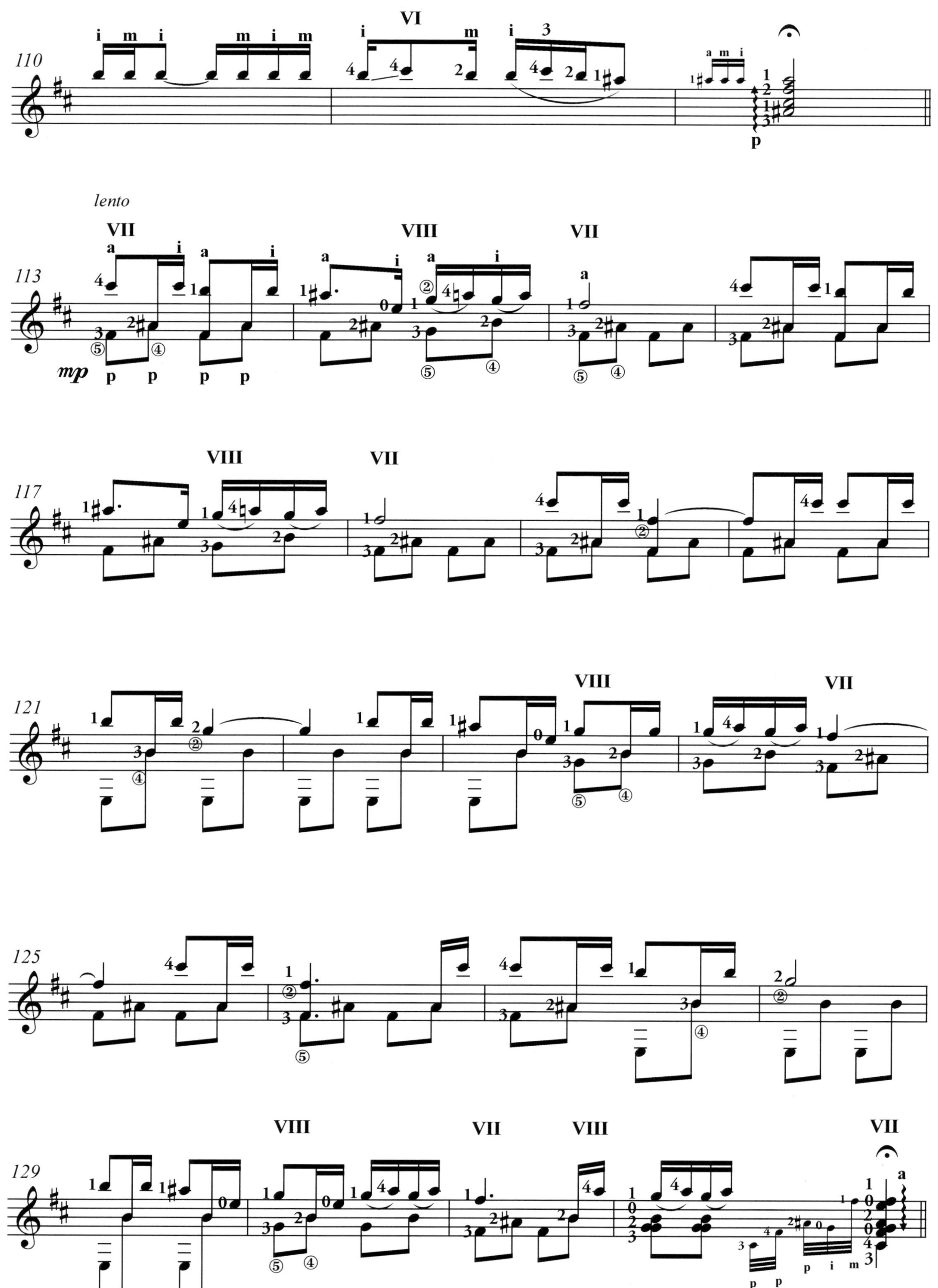
lento

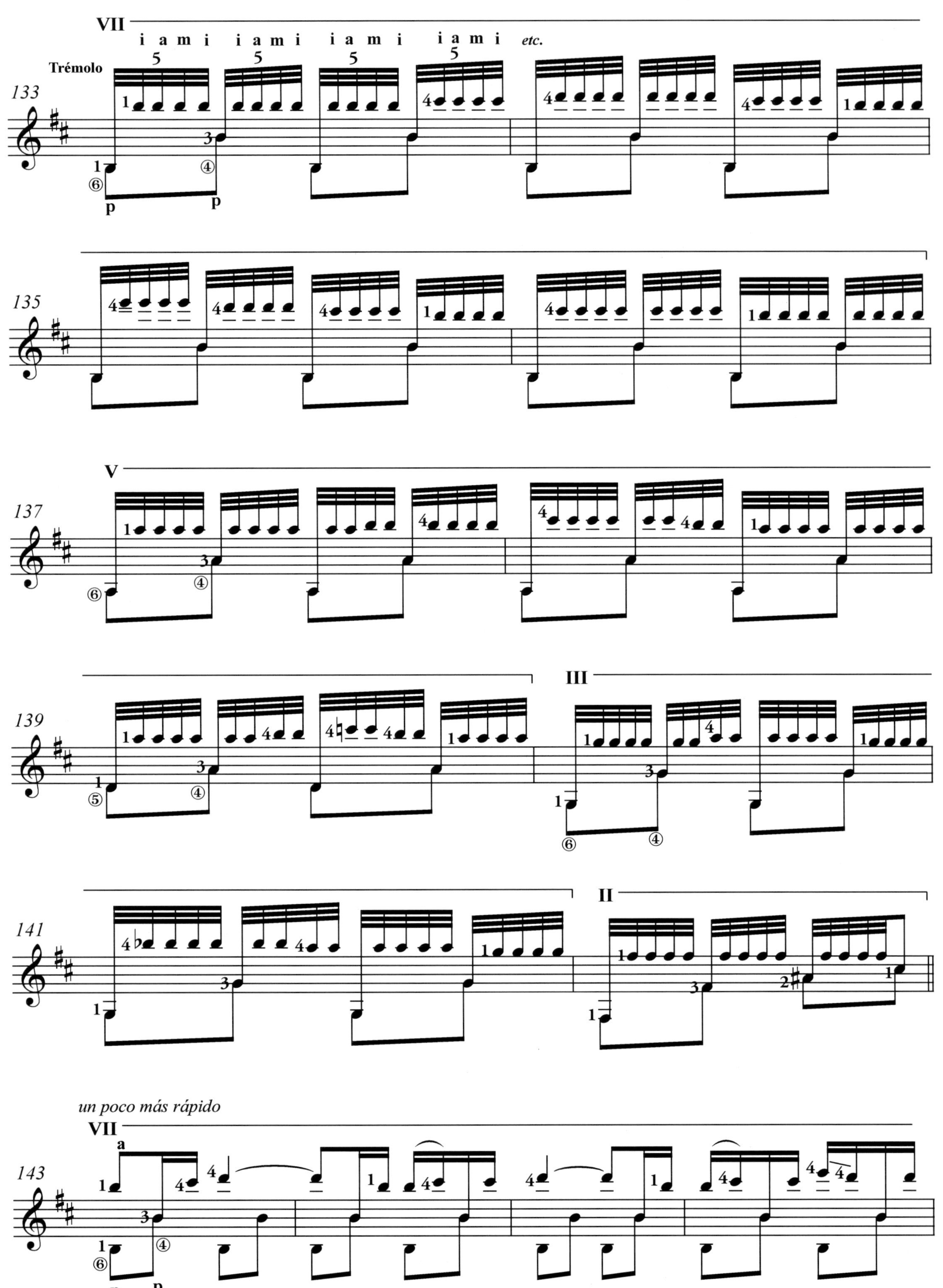
VII
i a m i i a m i i a m i i a m i etc.
Trémolo
133
135
V
137
139
III
141
II
un poco más rápido
VII
143

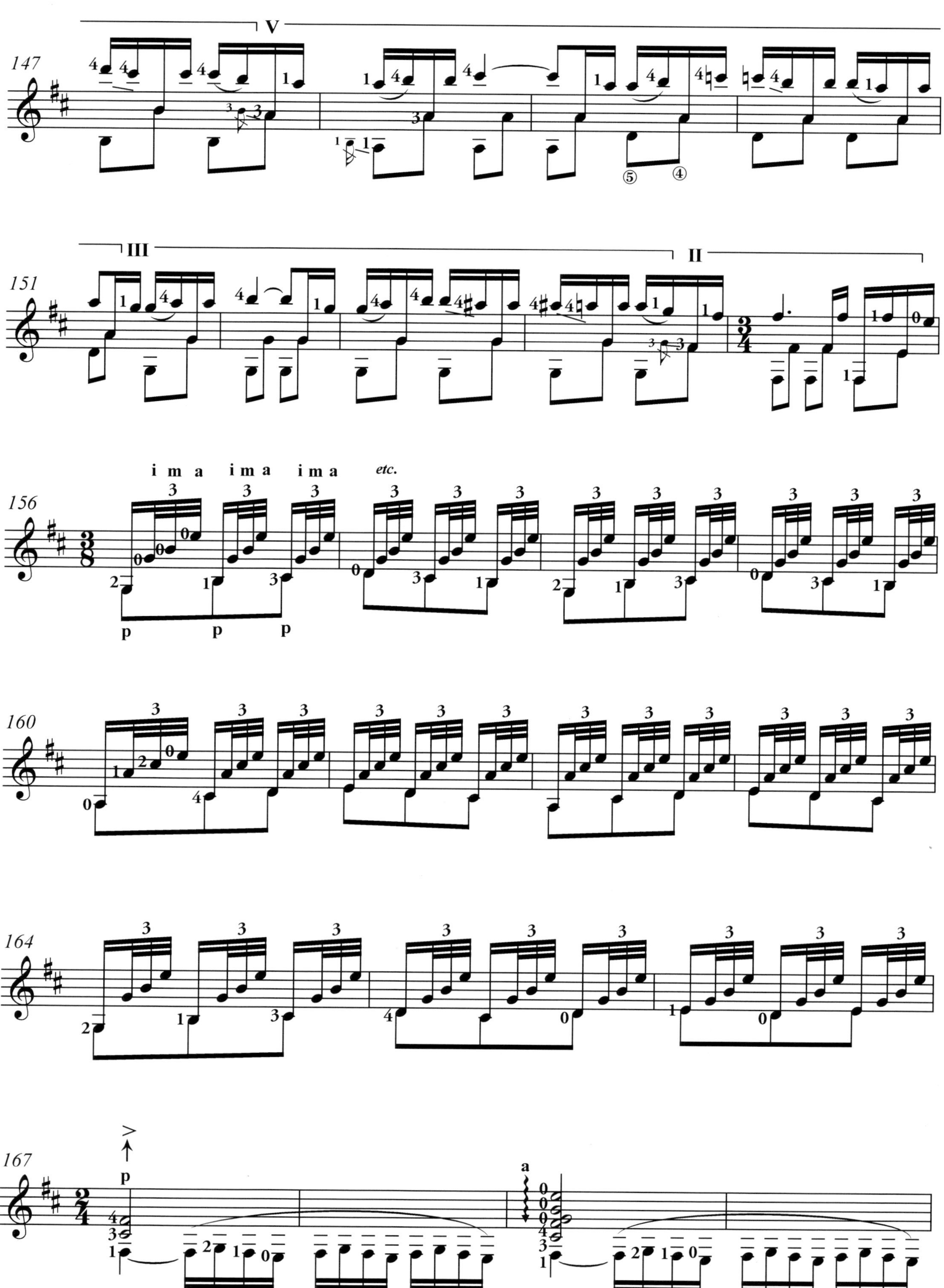
147
V
151
III
II
156
i m a
i m a
i m a
etc.
p
p
p
160
164
167
p
a

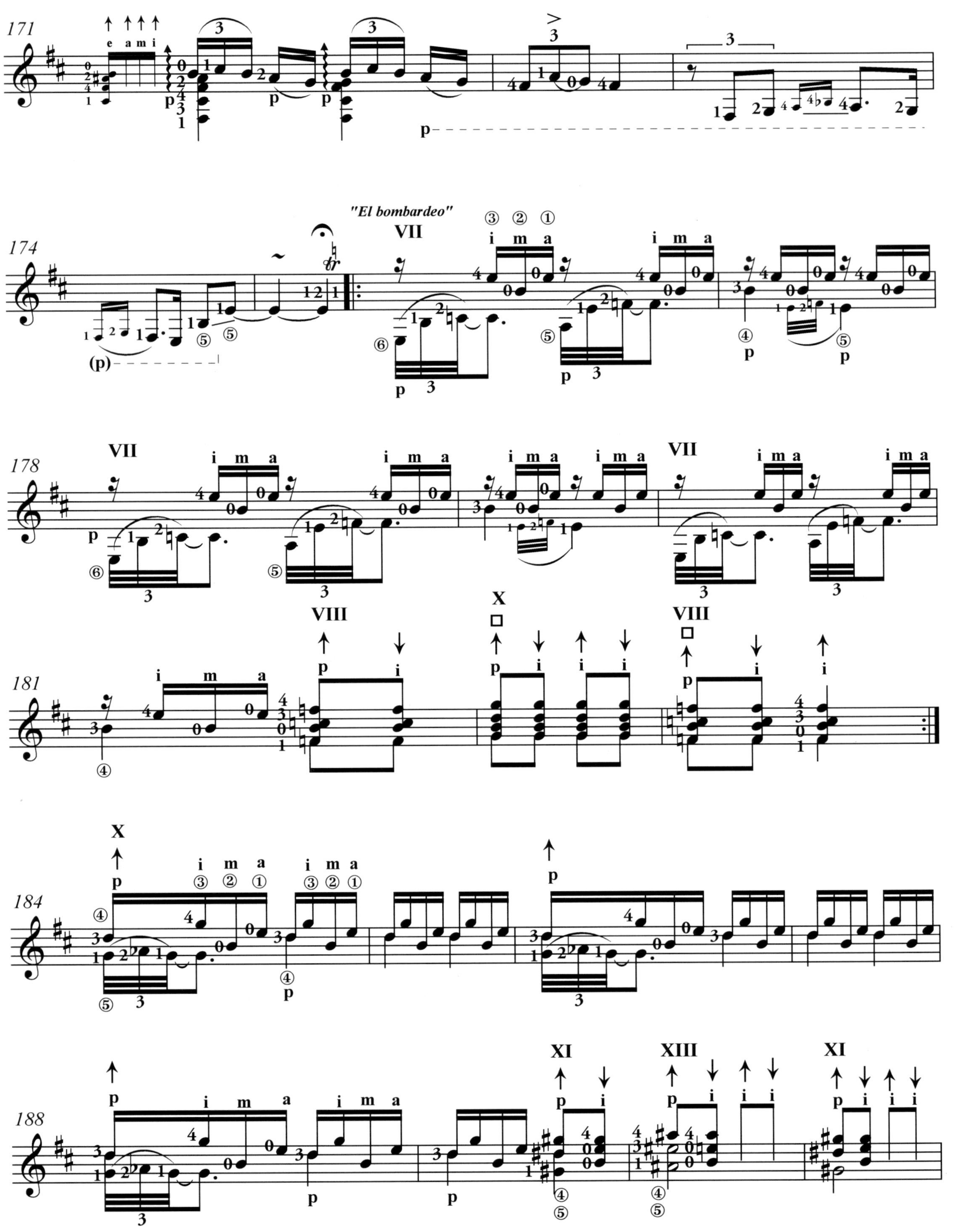
"El bombardeo"

192
X
196
XI
XIII
XIV
200
X
IX
204
VIII
208
VII
212
e a m

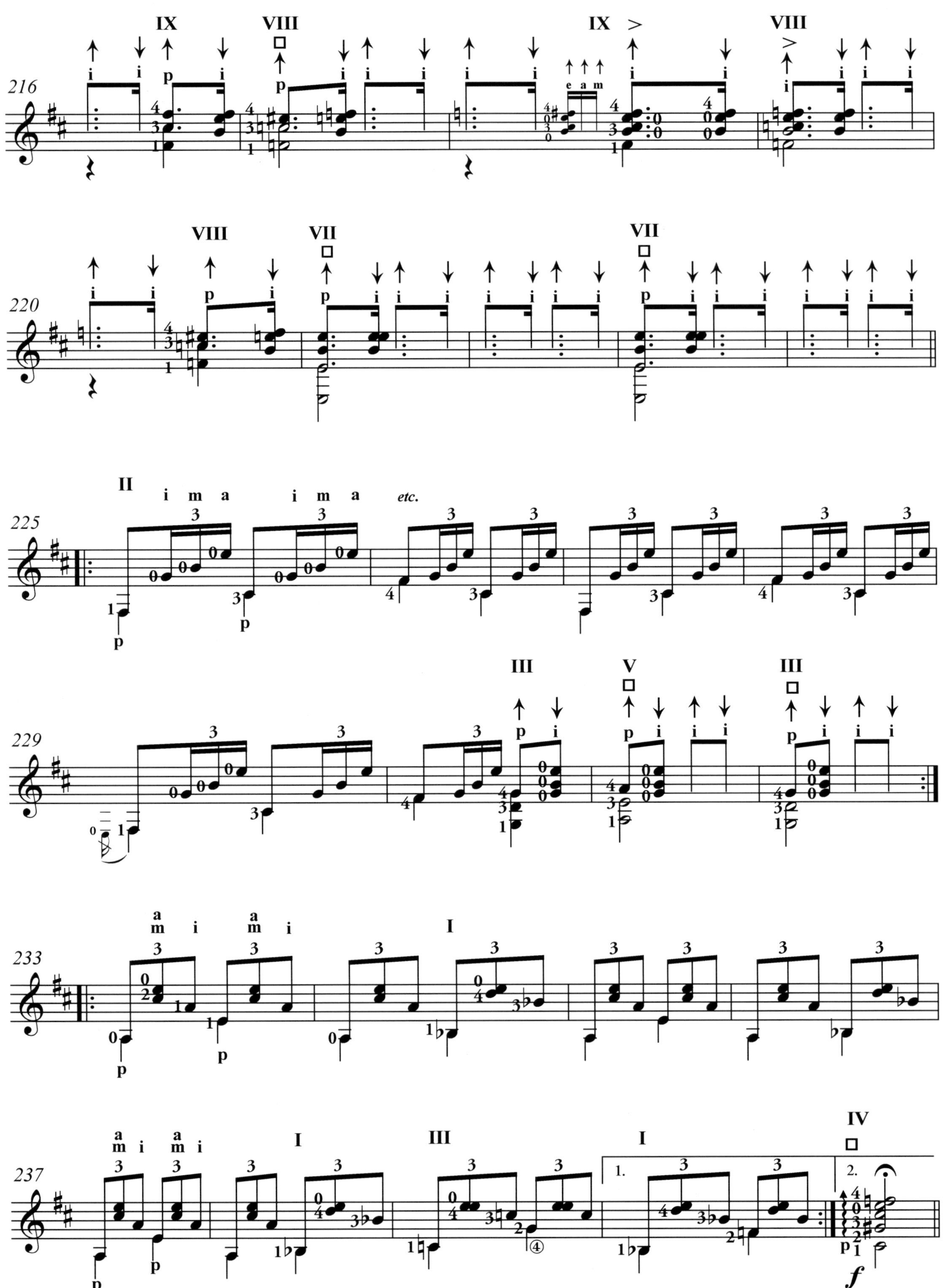
IX
VIII
IX
VIII
VII
VII
II
i m a
i m a
etc.
III
V
III
a
m i
a
m i
I
I
III
I
IV
1.
2.

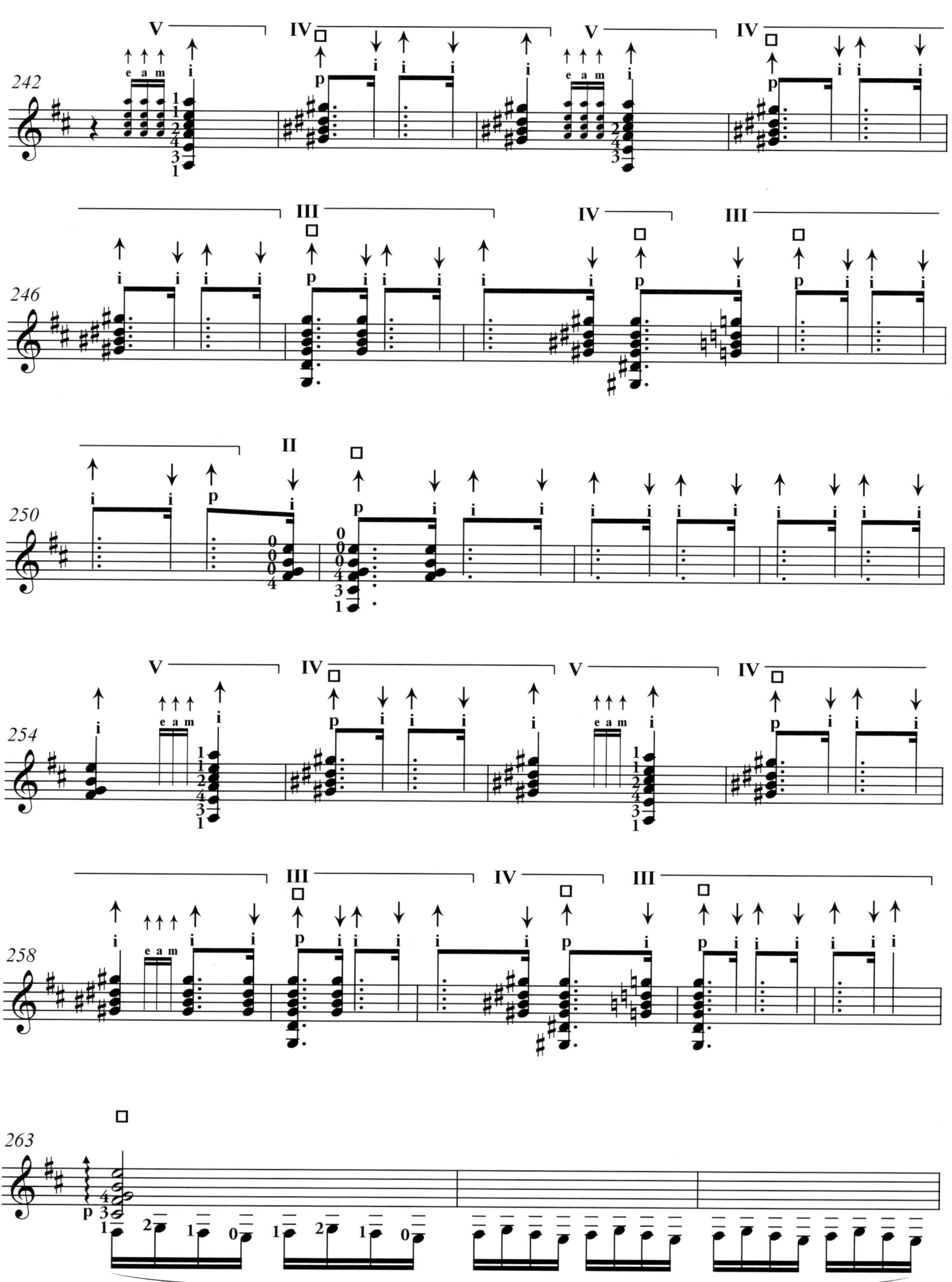
242
V
IV
V
IV
246
III
IV
III
250
II
254
V
IV
V
IV
258
III
IV
III
263

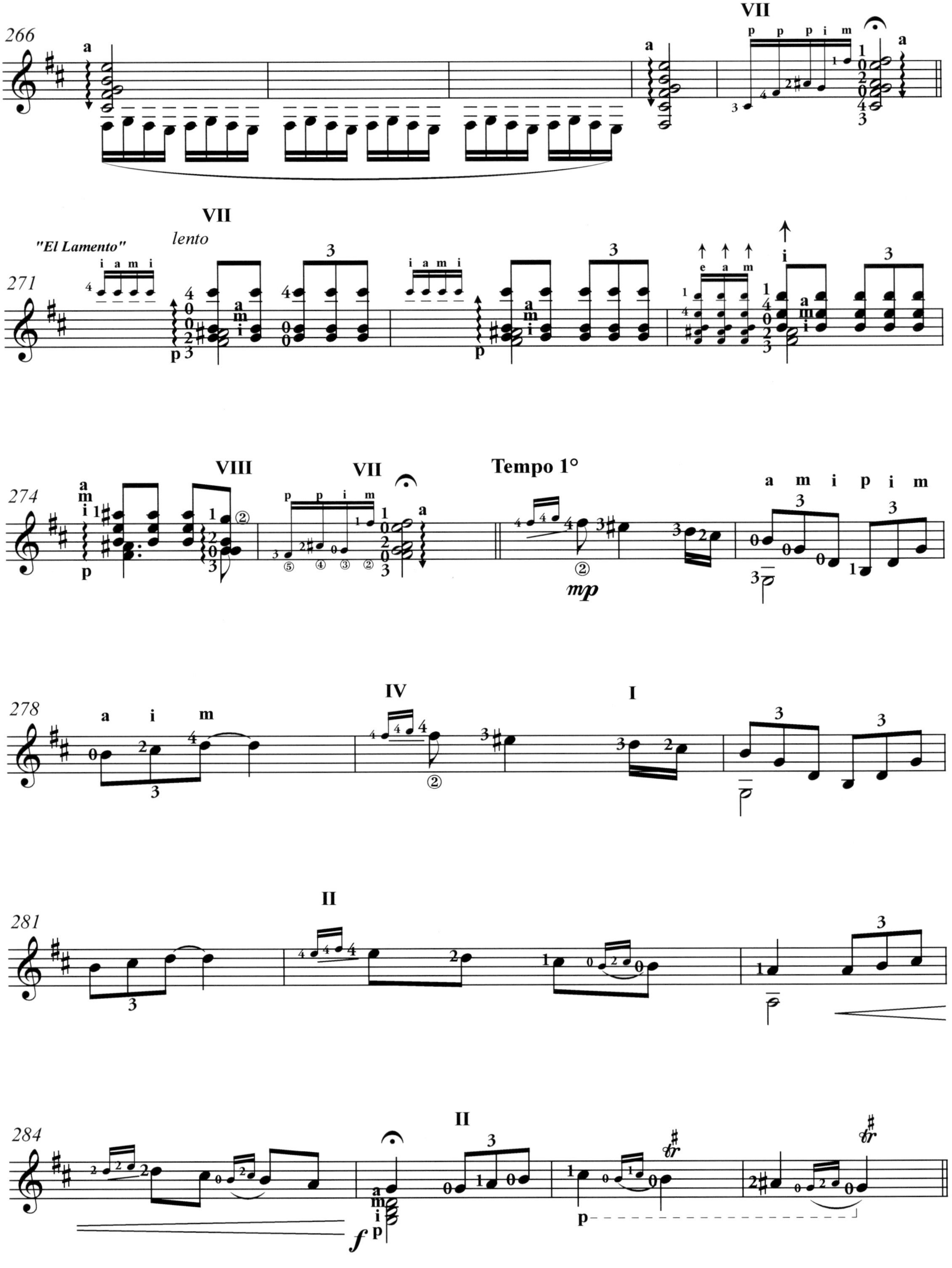

266 a VII p p p i m a

271 "El Lamento" VII *lento* i a m i

274 VIII VII Tempo 1° a m i p i m *mp*

278 a i m IV I

281 II

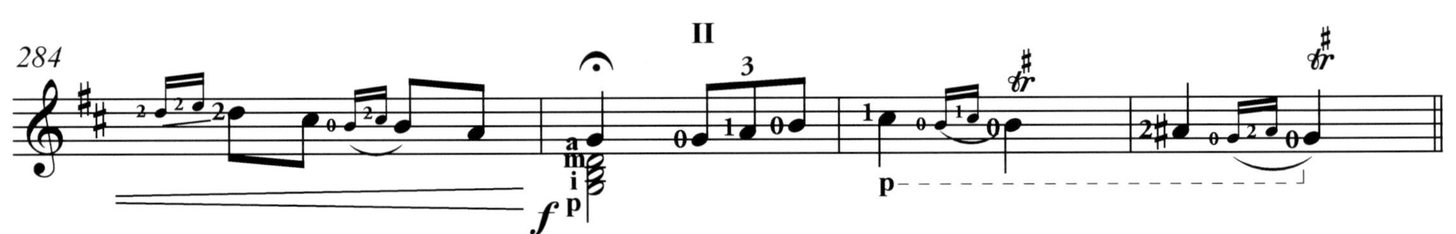

288
292
296
300
304
mp
308
rall...
p

Alegría de Pablo

Transcription by
ANGELA CENTOLA

JUAN MARTÍN

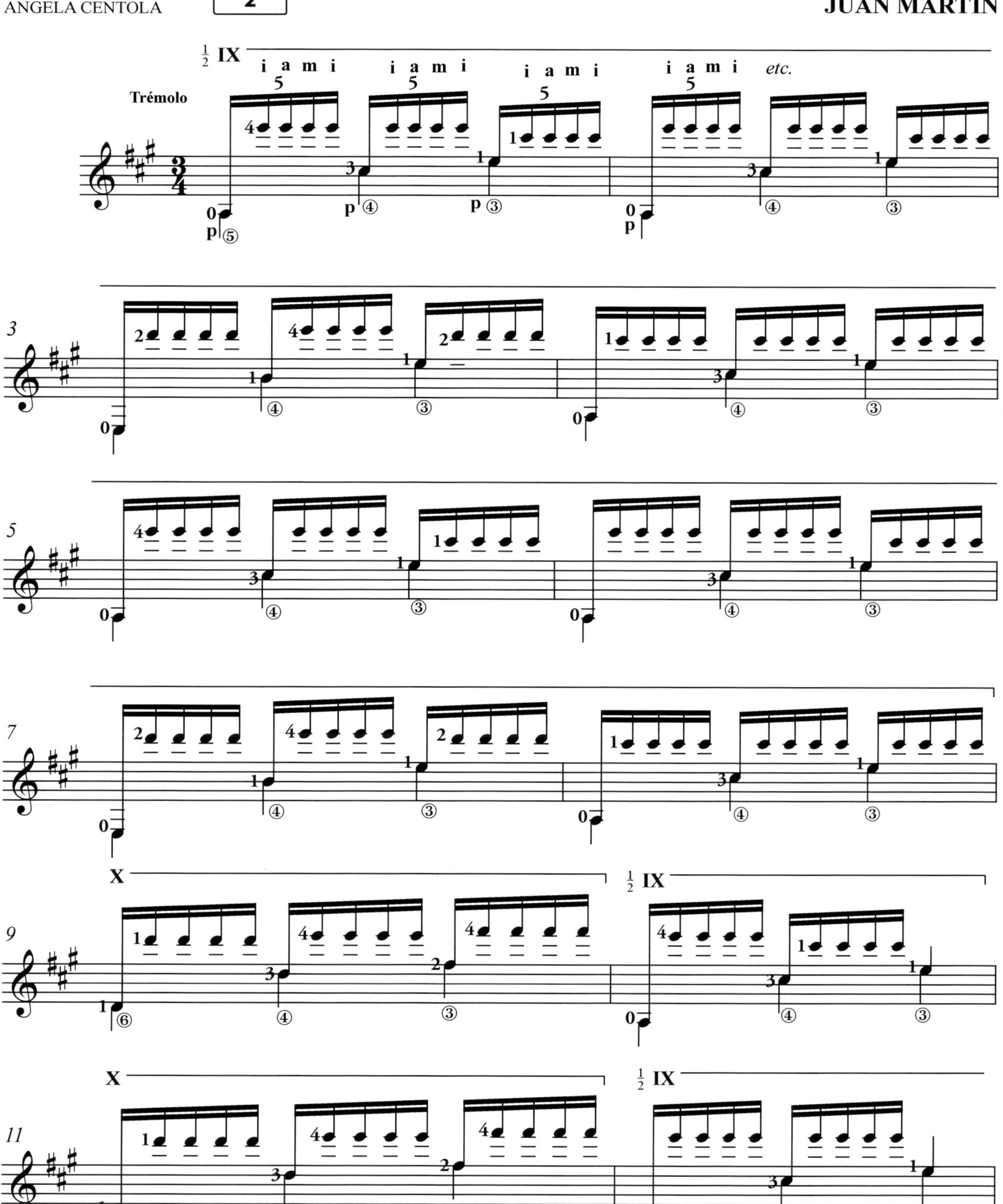

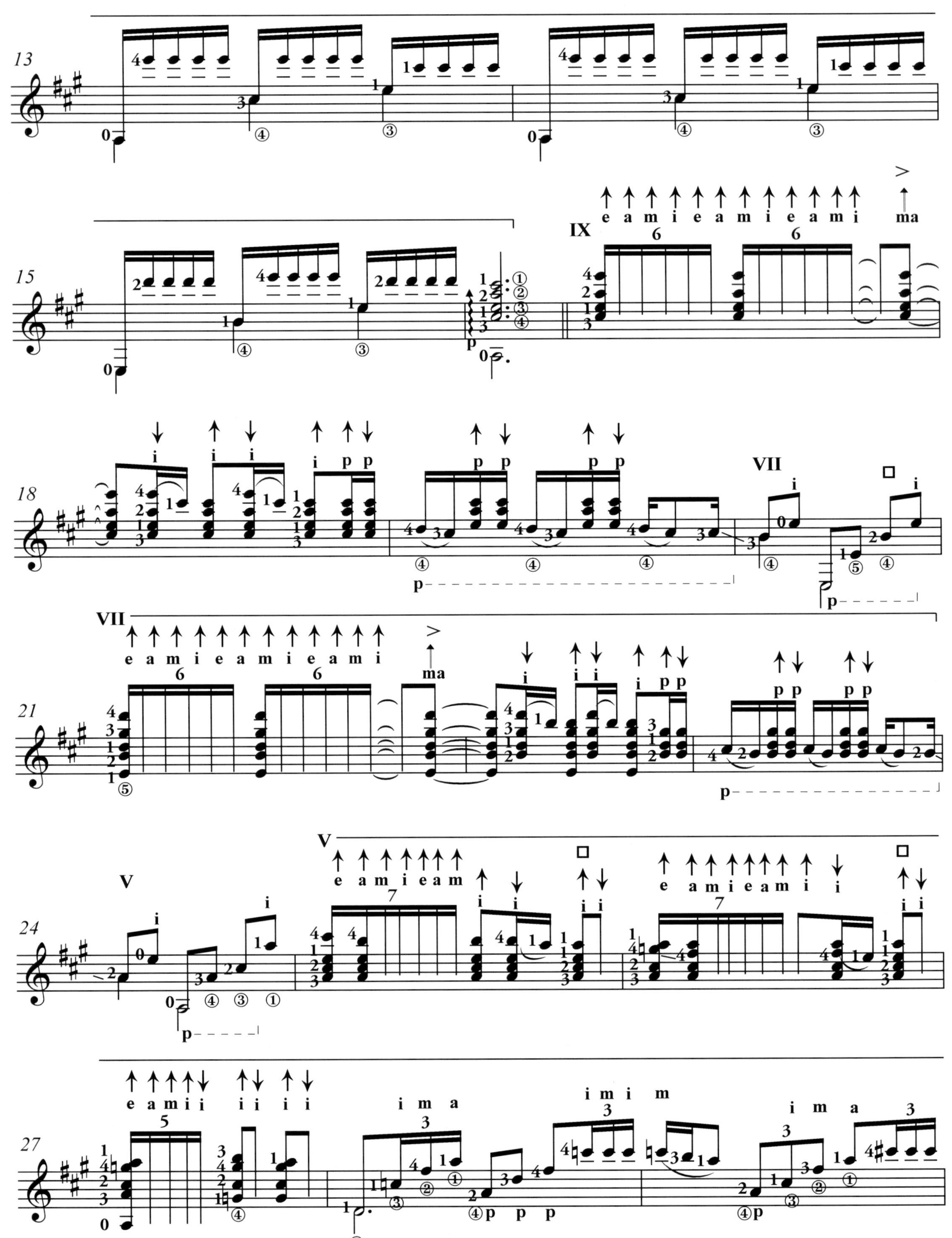
13
15
IX
e a m i e a m i e a m i
ma
18
VII
21
e a m i e a m i e a m i
ma
24
V
27
e a m i i
i m a
i m i m

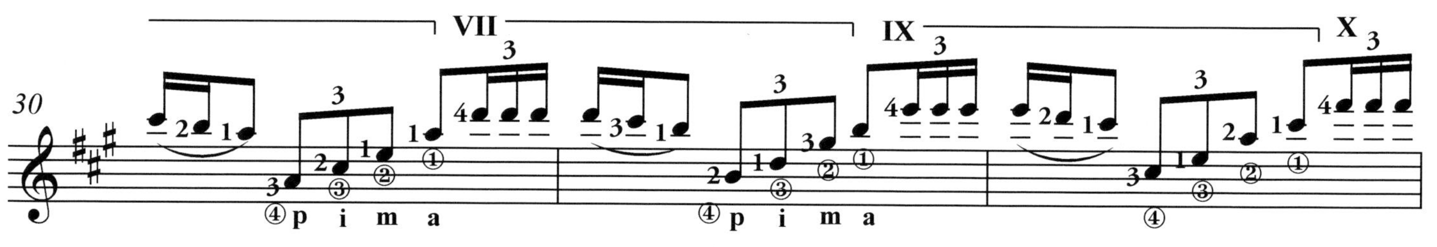
30
VII
IX
X
p i m a
p i m a

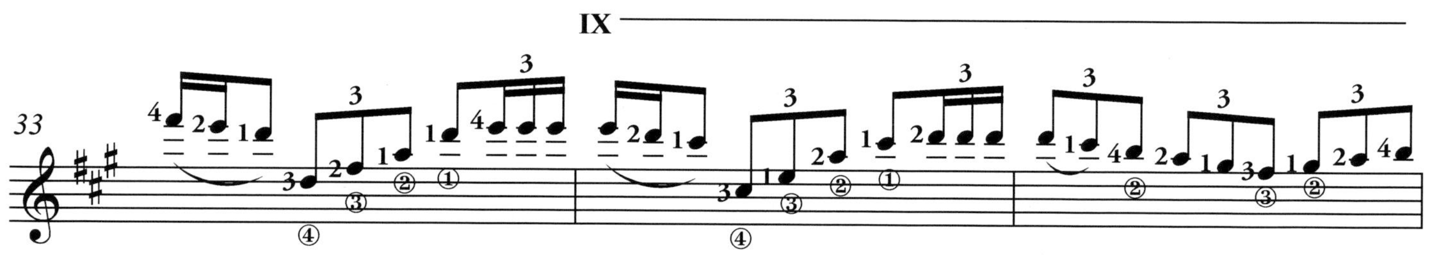
33
IX

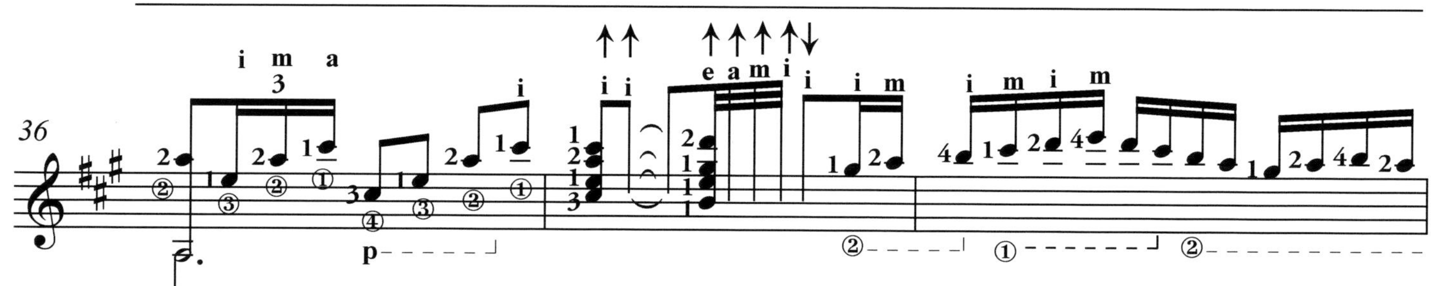
36
i m a
e a m i
i m
i m i m

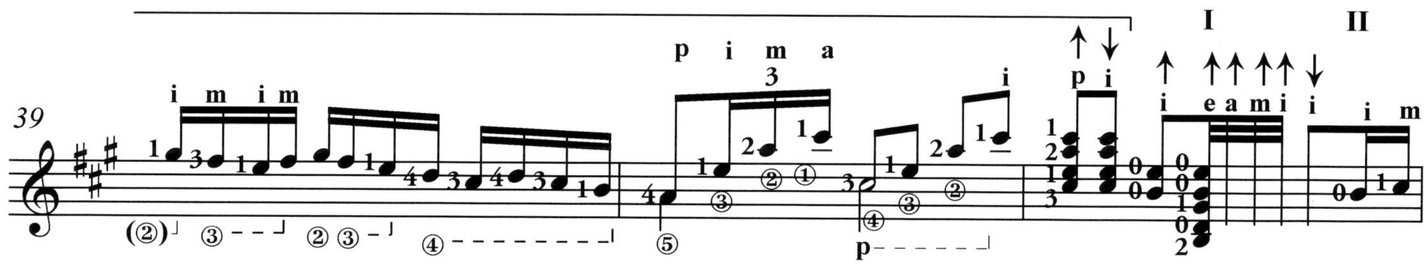
39
i m i m
p i m a
I
II
e a m i
i m

42
i m i m
I

45
½ II

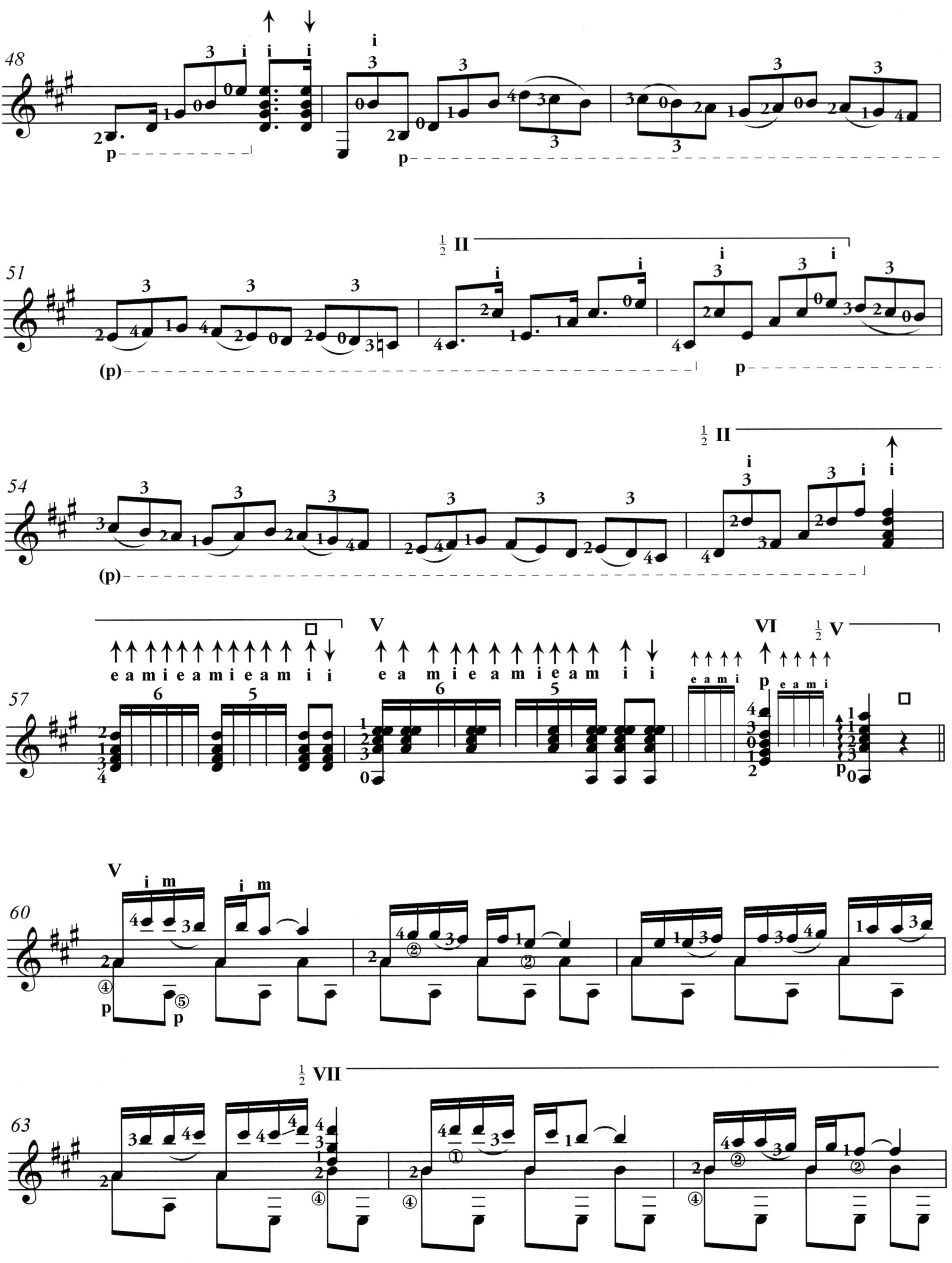

½ IX
X
IX
X
IX
IX
½ IX
rallentando
a tiempo
IX

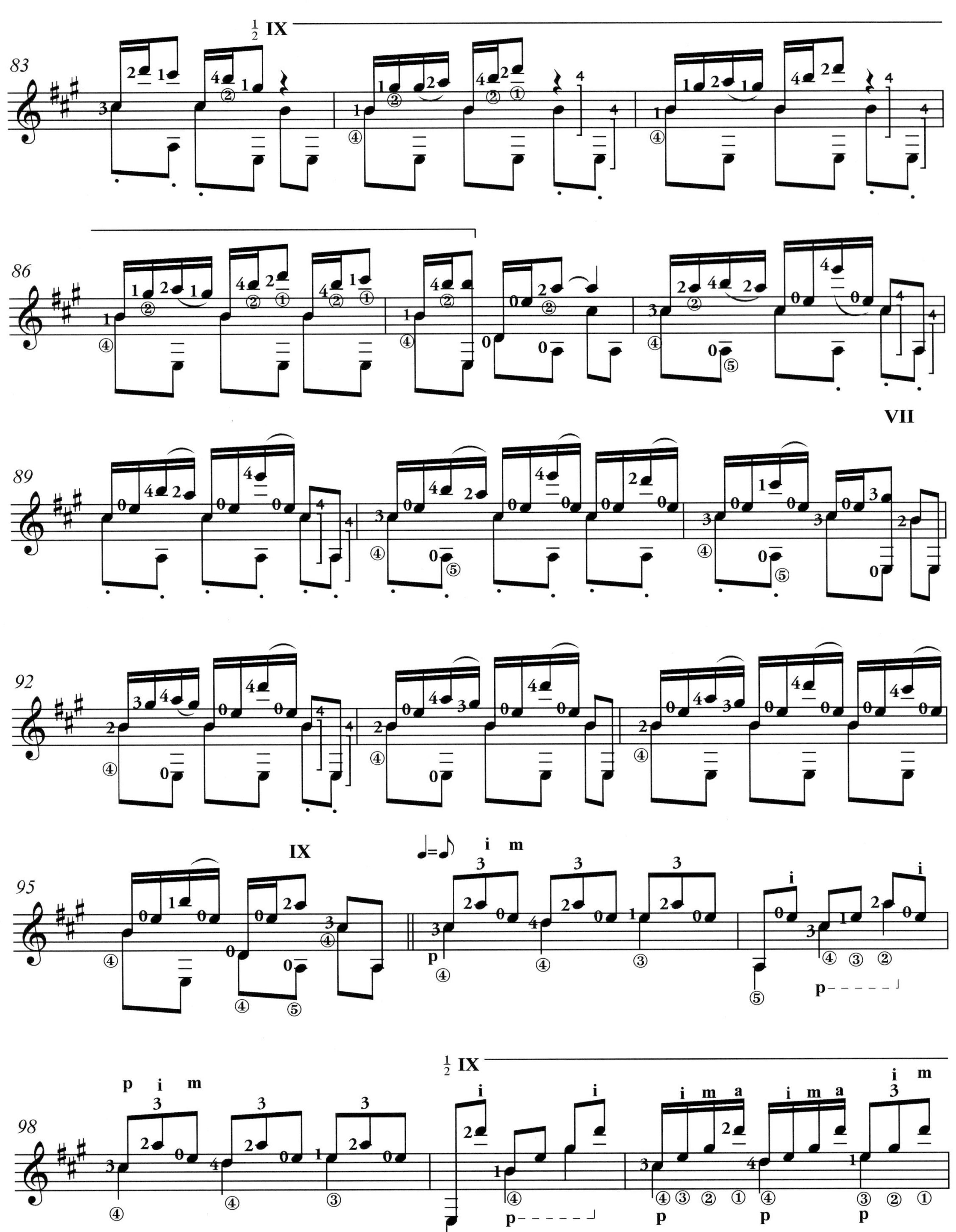
83
½ IX
86
89
VII
92
95
IX
i m
98
p i m
½ IX
i m a

121
X
124
½ IX
127
X
½ IX
130
132
½ IX
e a m i
135
VII
VI

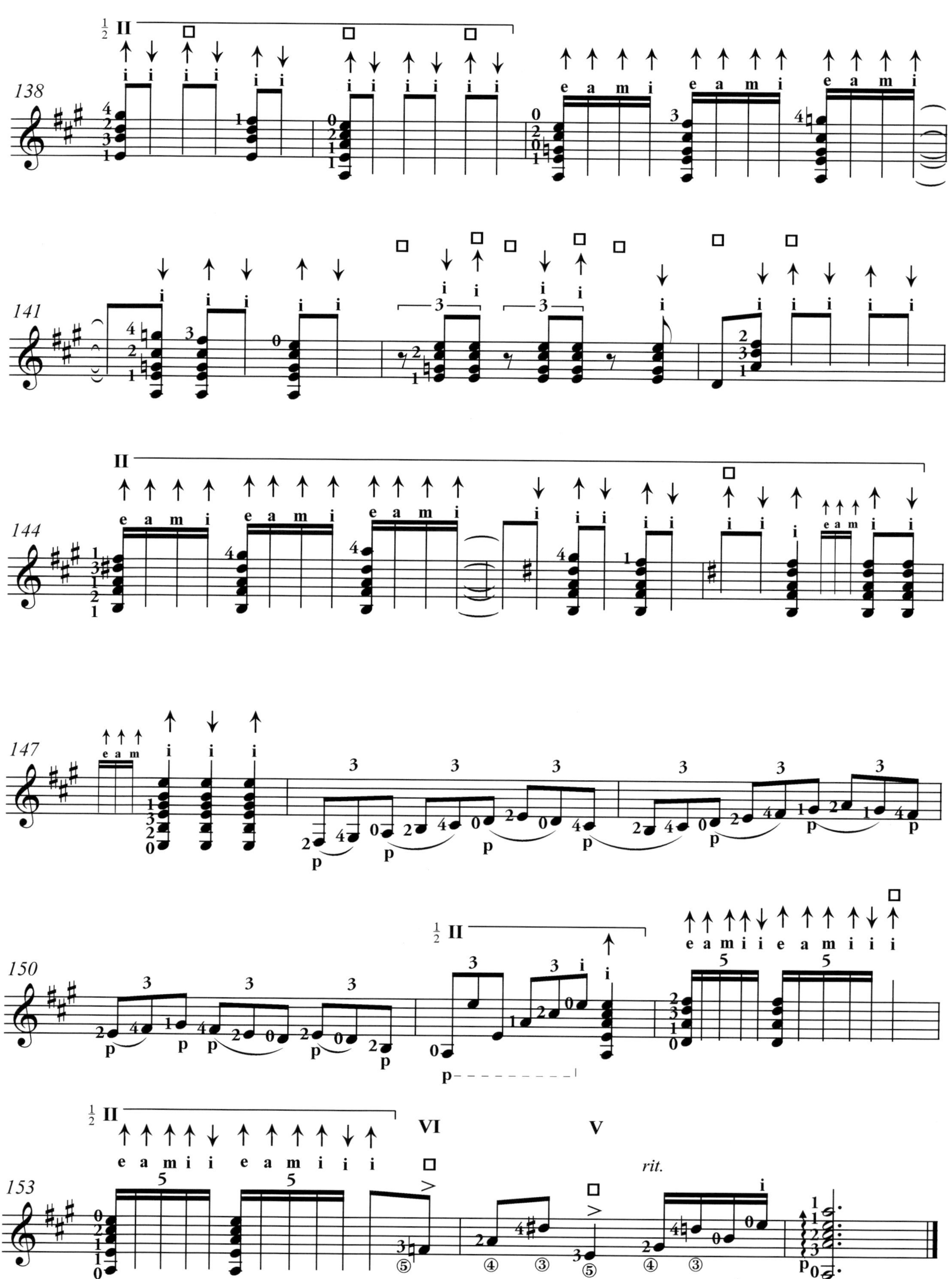
rit.

Farruca Martín

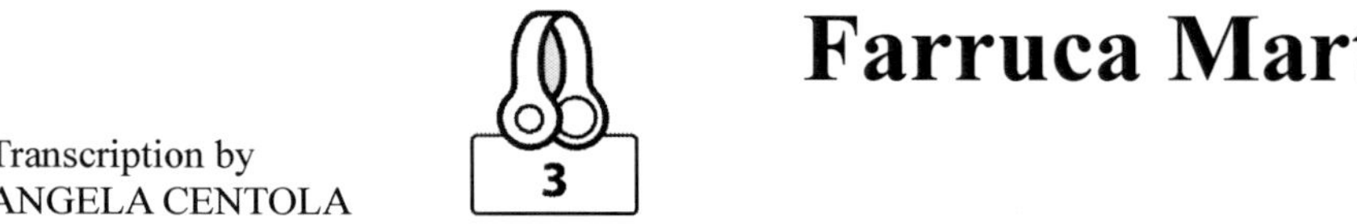

Transcription by
ANGELA CENTOLA

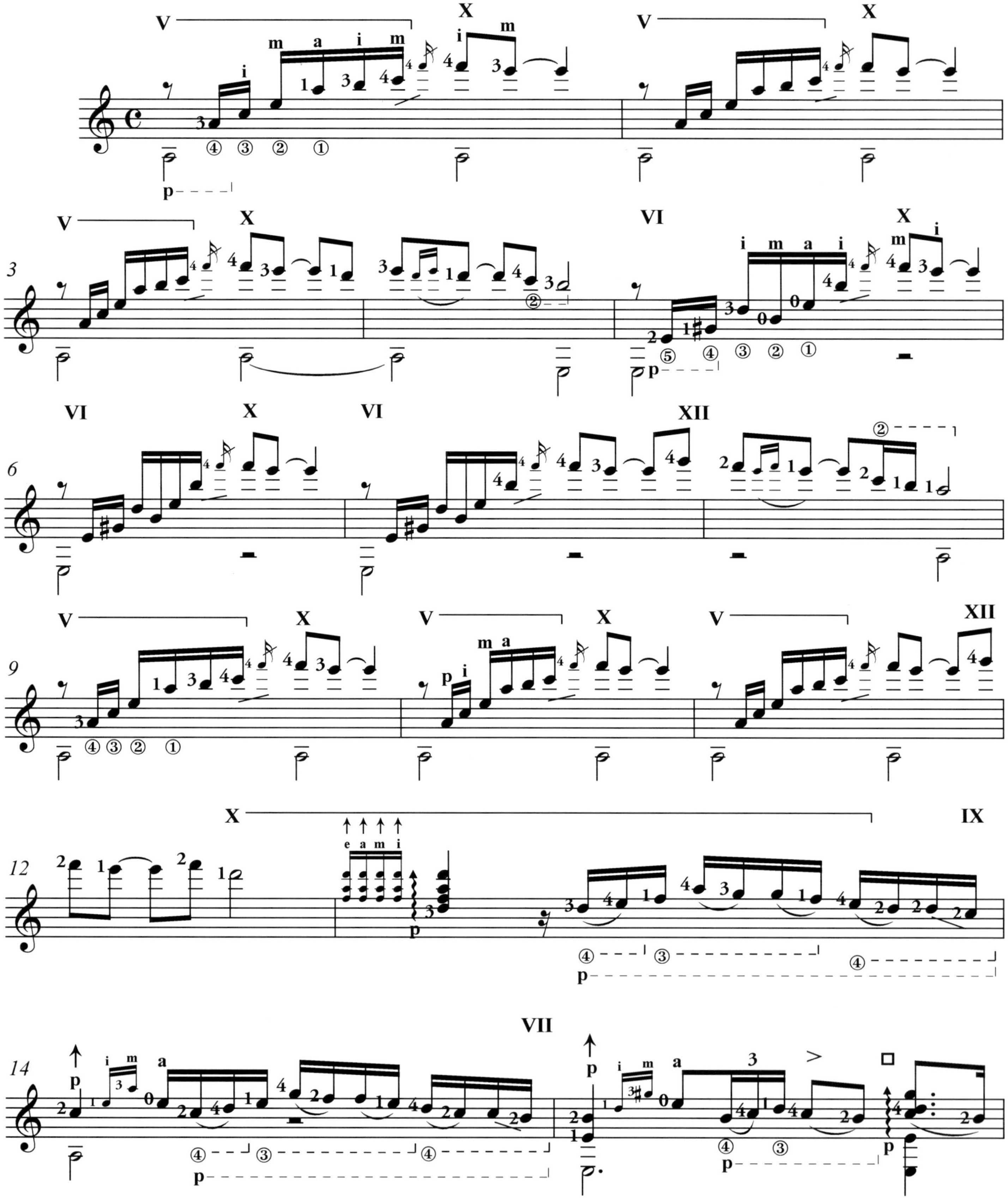

JUAN MARTÍN

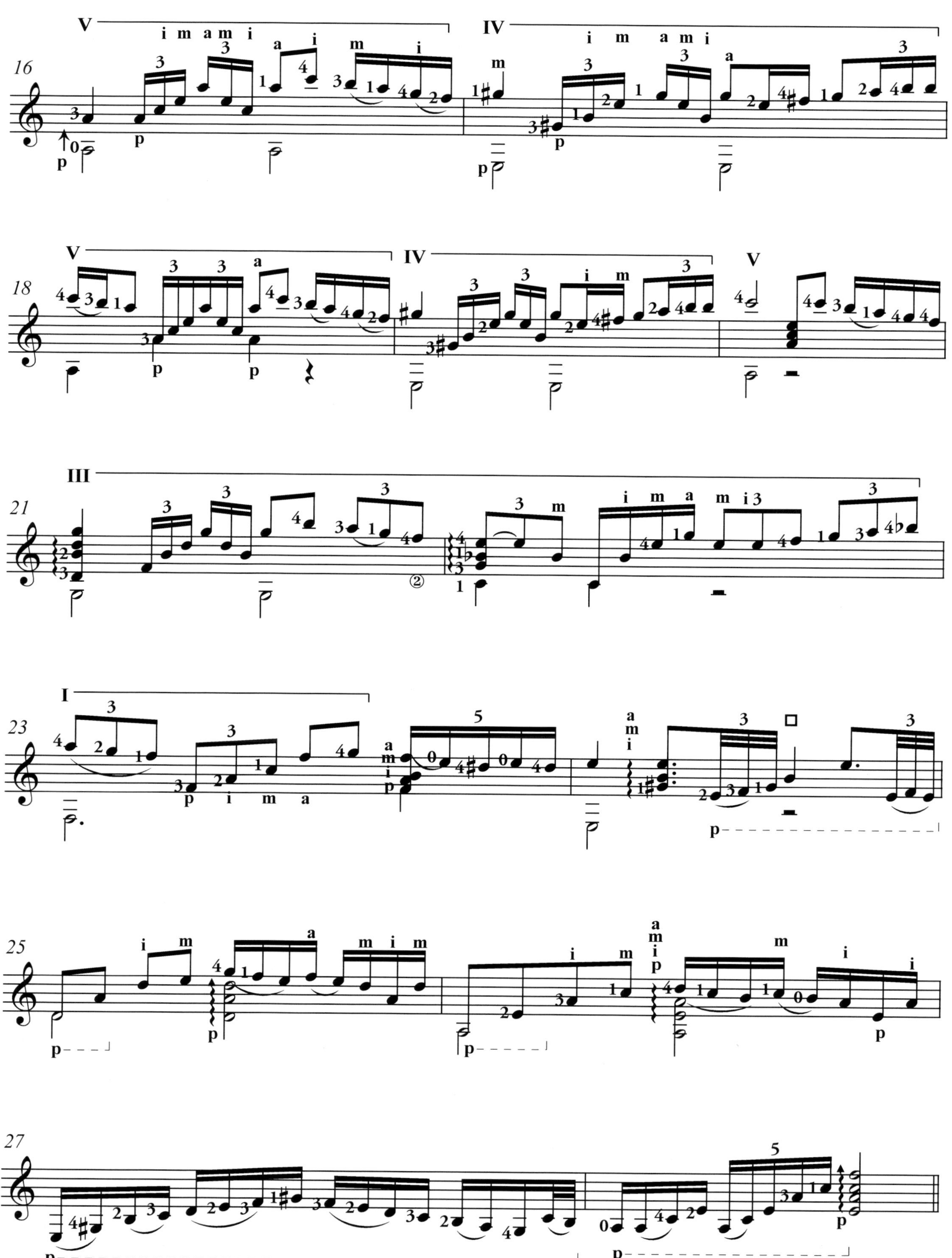

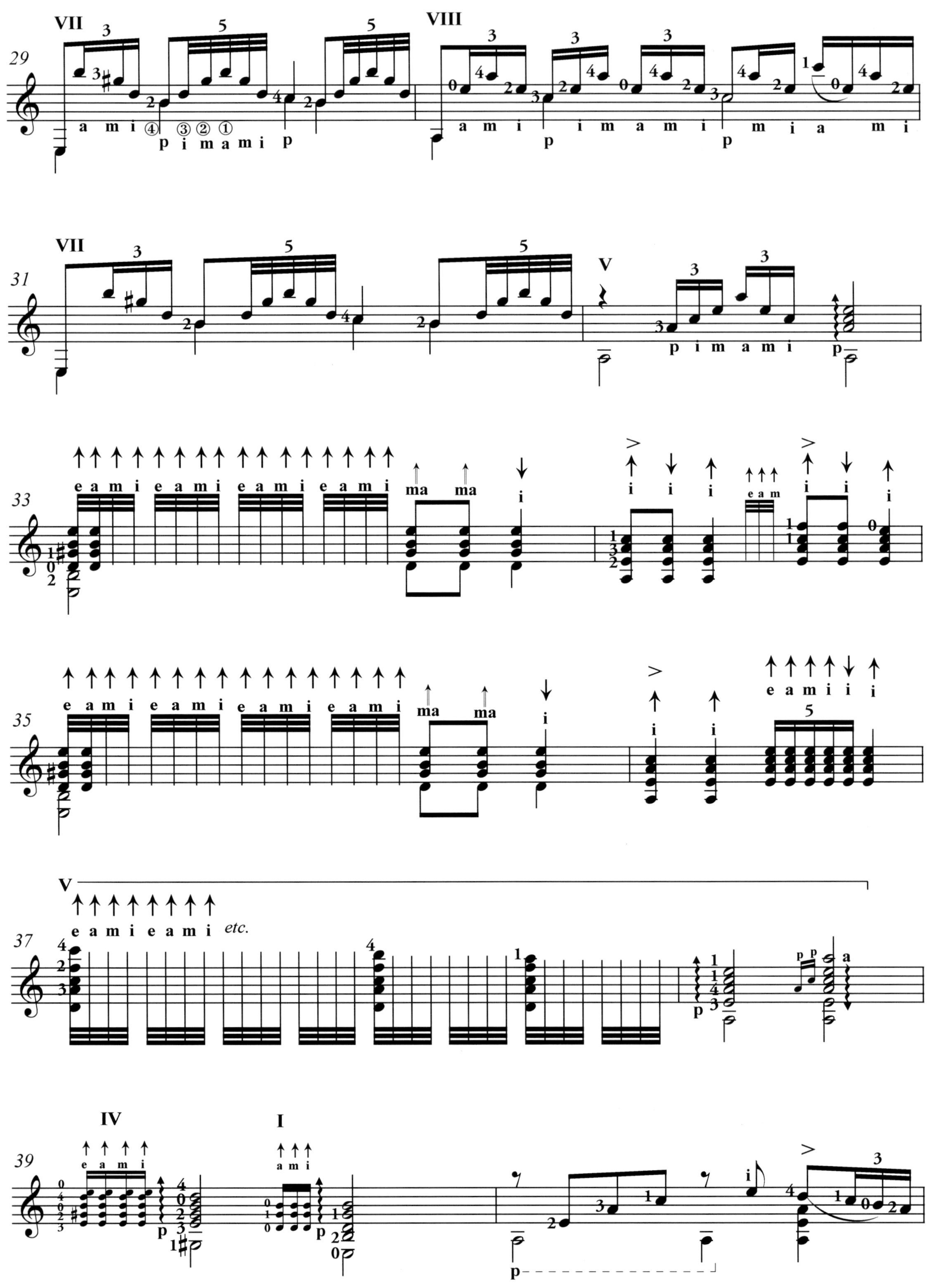
VII
VIII
a m i p i m a m i p
a m i p i m a m i p m i a m i
VII
V
p i m a m i p
e a m i e a m i e a m i e a m i
ma ma i
i i i e a m i i i
e a m i e a m i e a m i e a m i
ma ma i
i i e a m i i i
V
e a m i e a m i etc.
p p p a
IV
e a m i
p
I
a m i
p
i
p

X
IX
VII
VIII
p
i m i m i m
Trémolo
½ V
i a m i
etc.
VI
V

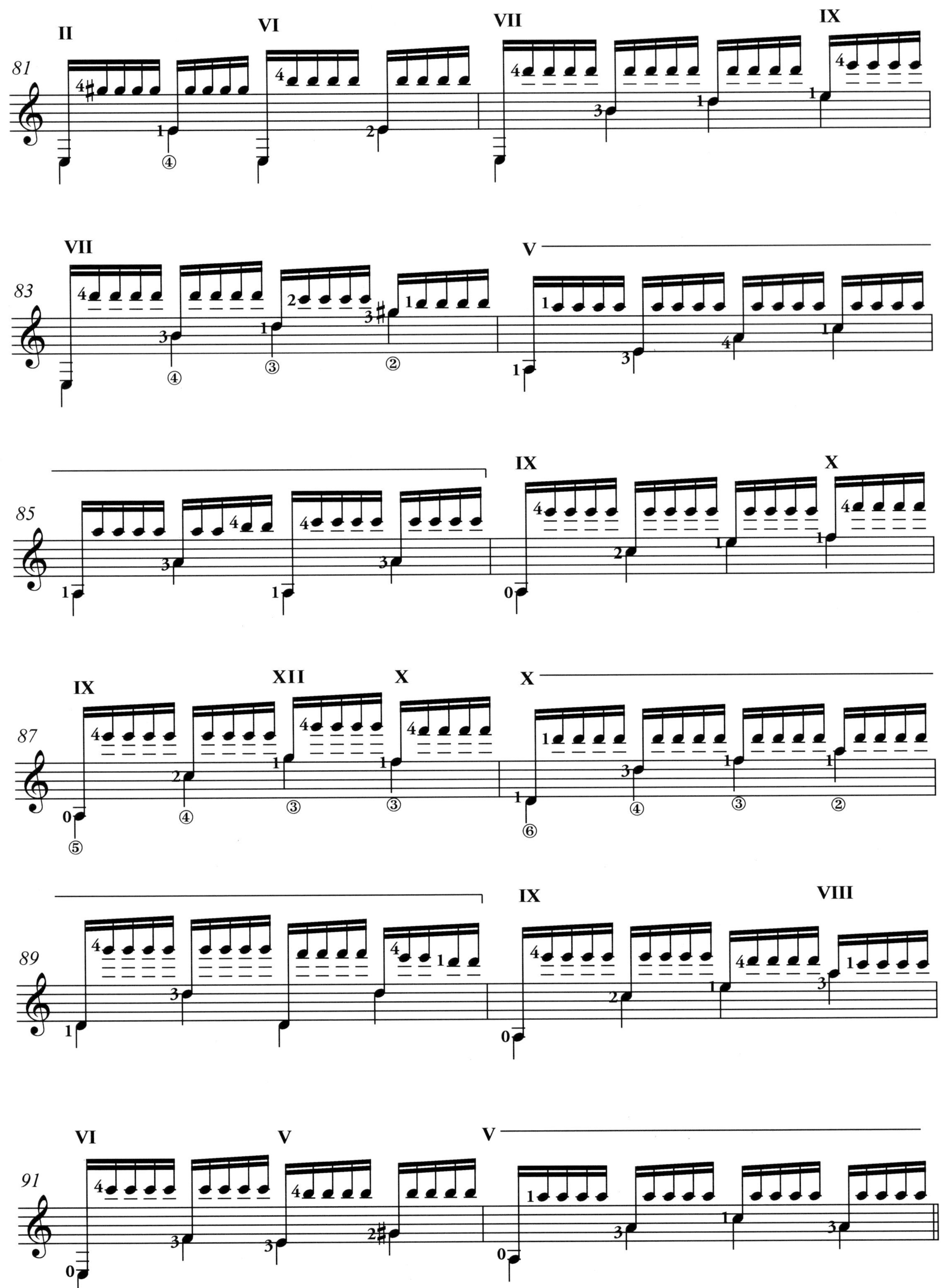

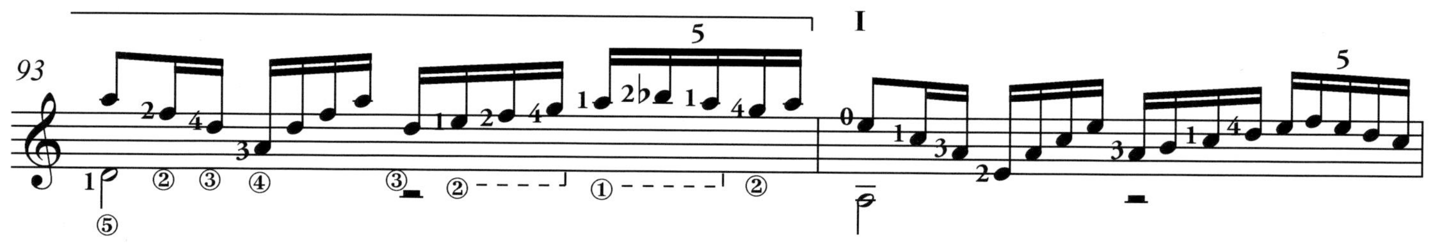

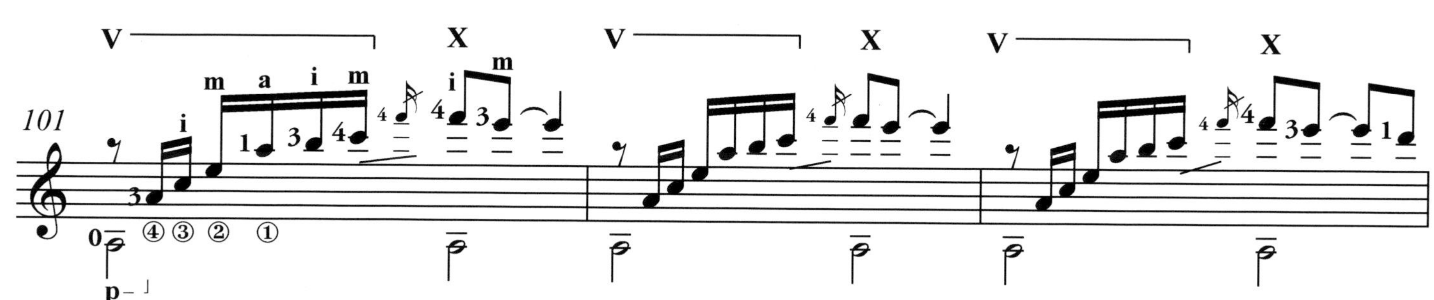
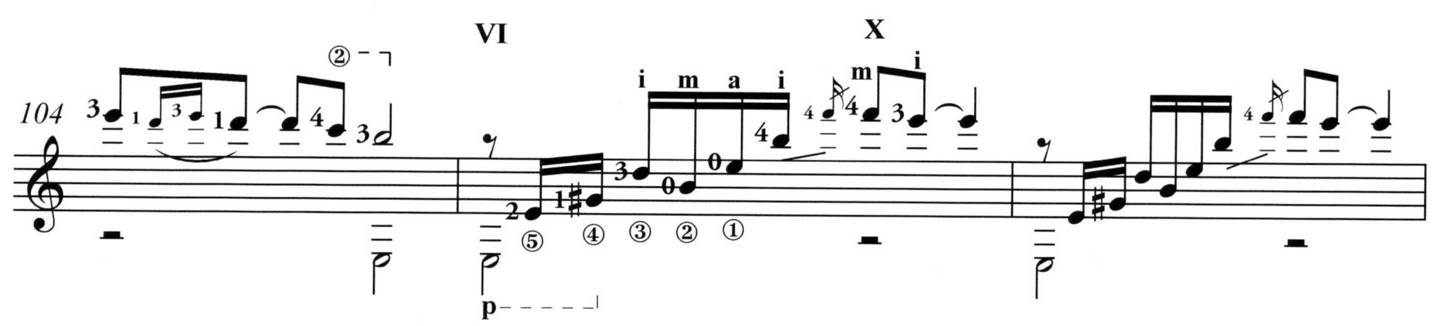
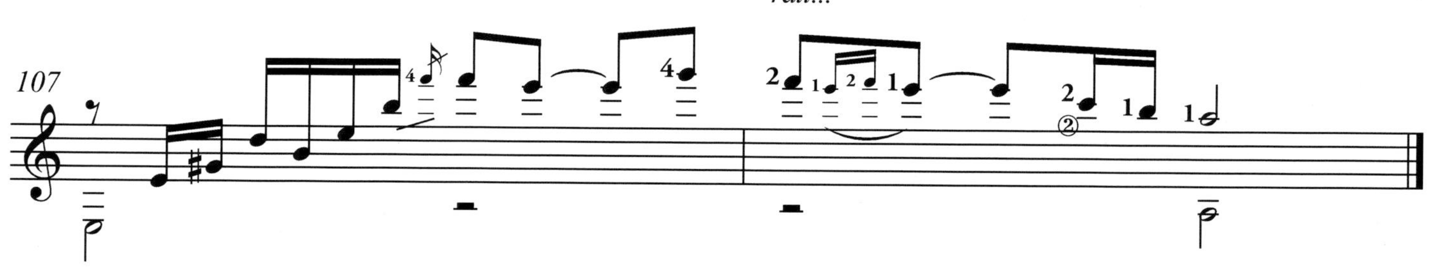
rall...

El deseo atrapado por la cola

Transcription by
ANGELA CENTOLA

4

Rumba

JUAN MARTÍN

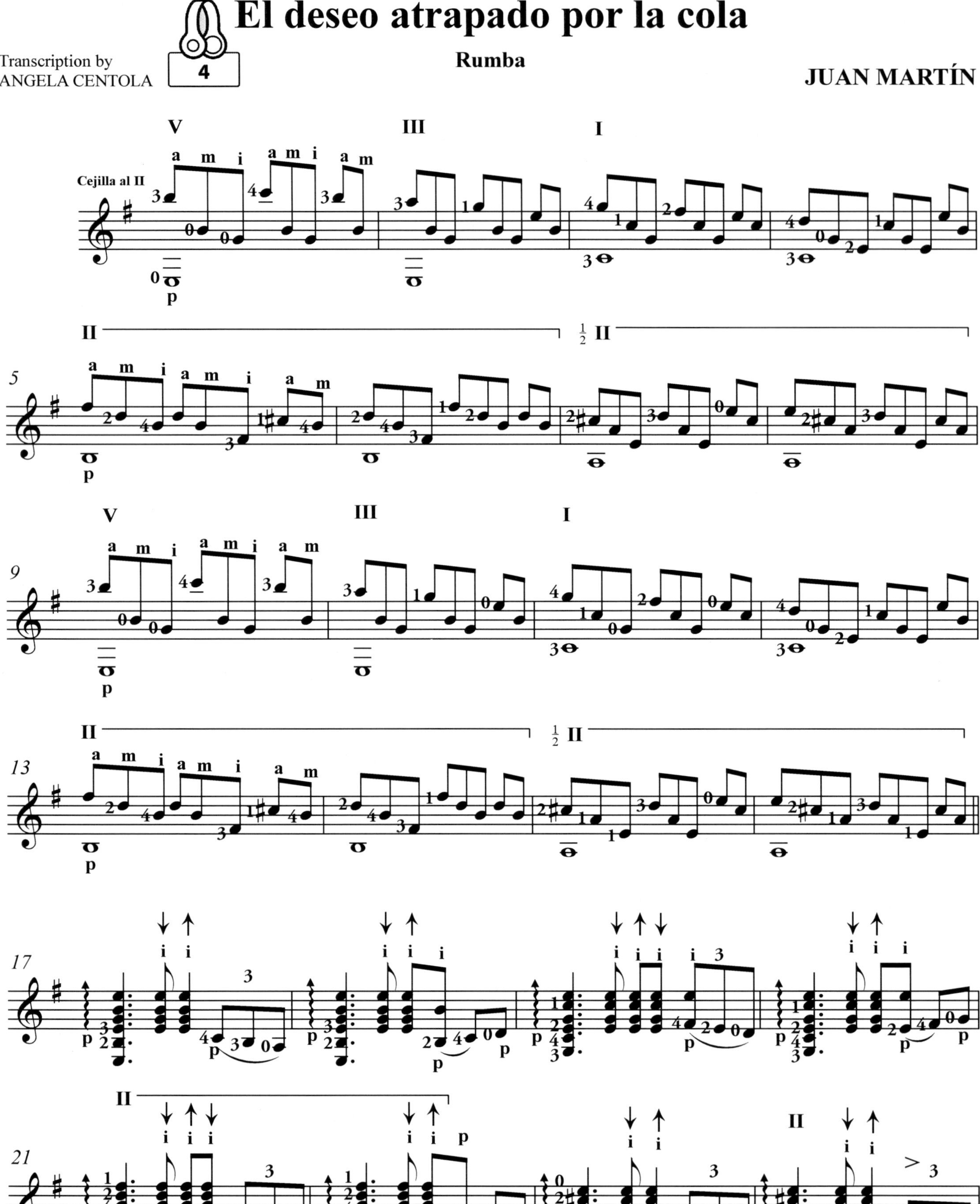

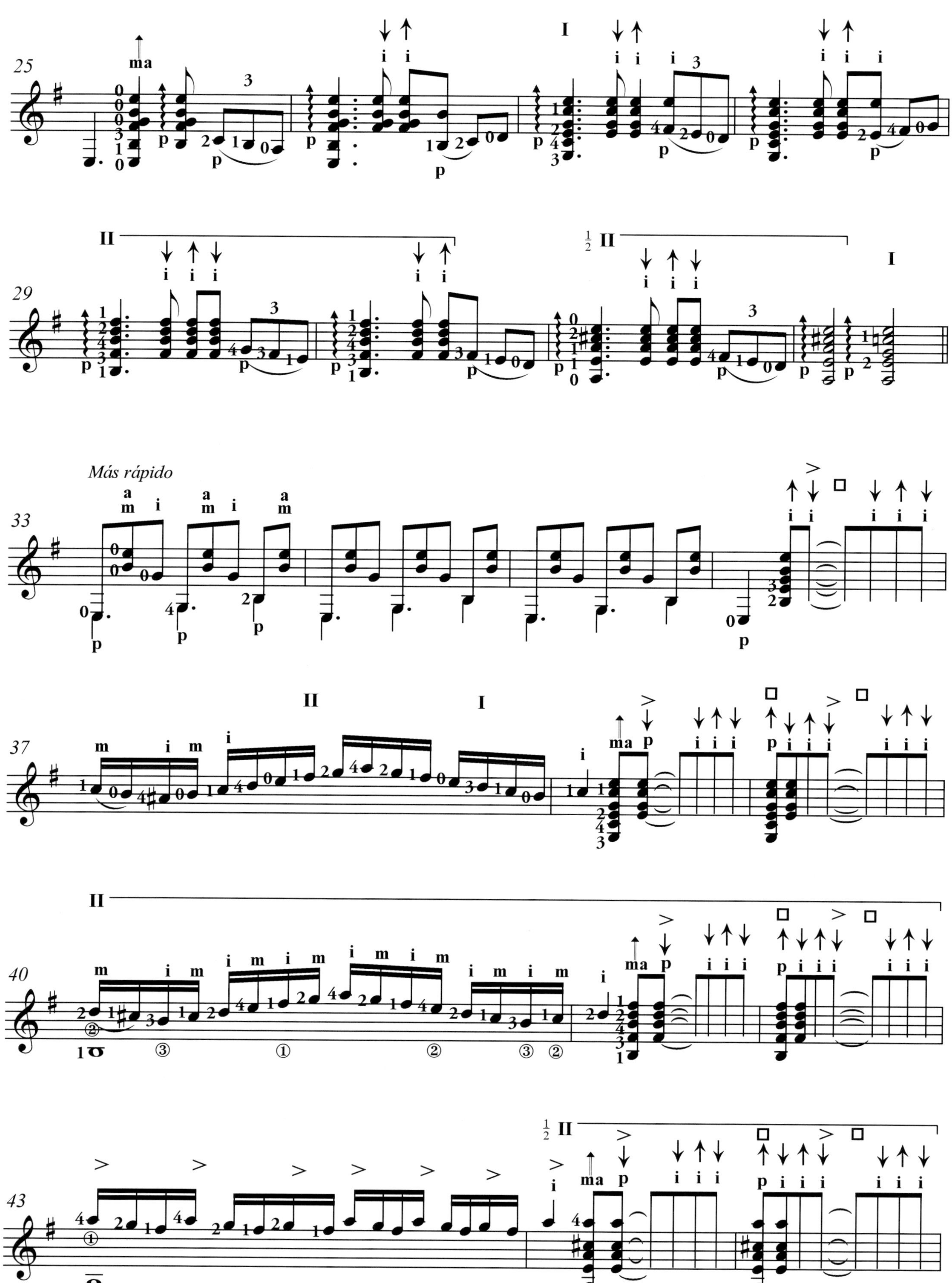
Más rápido

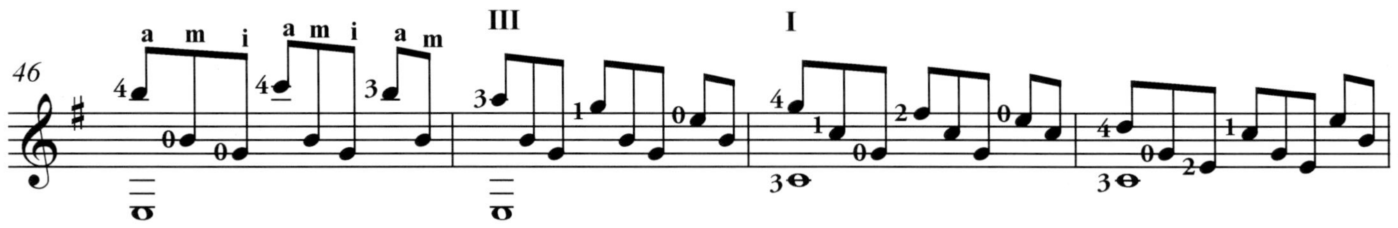
46
III
I

50
II
½ II

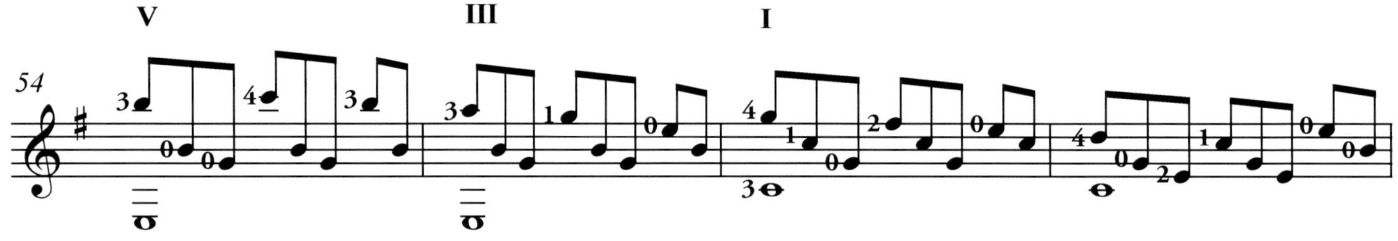
54
V
III
I

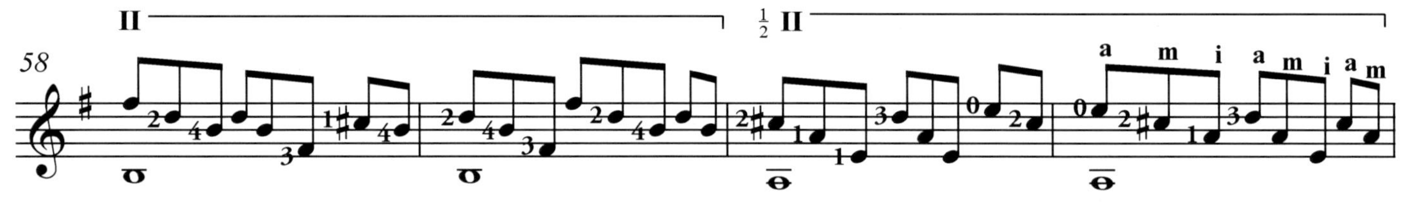
58
II
½ II

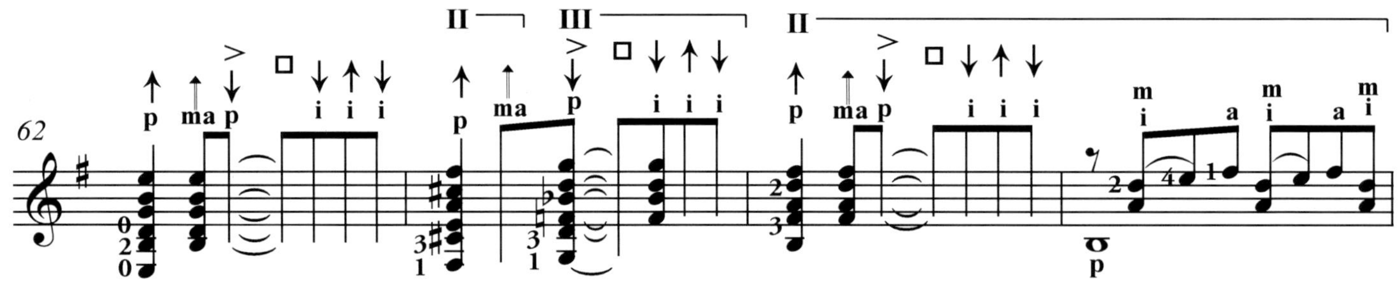
62
II
III
II

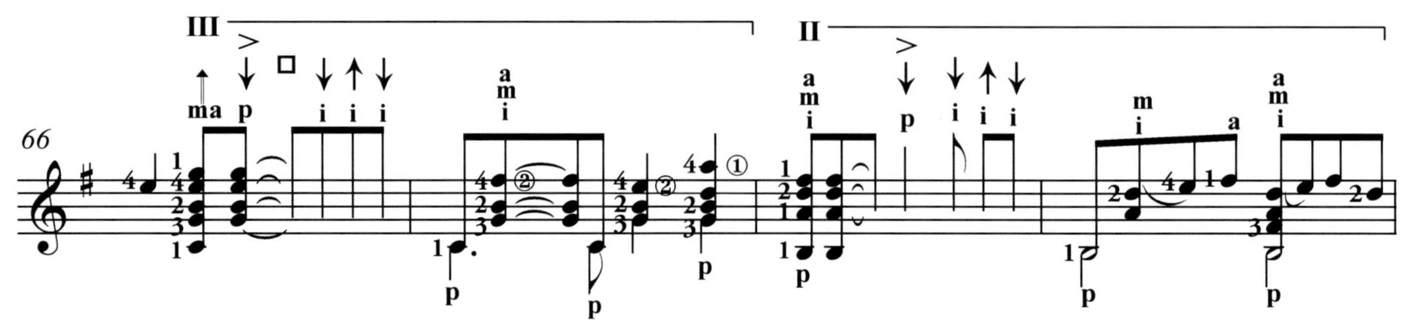
66
III
II

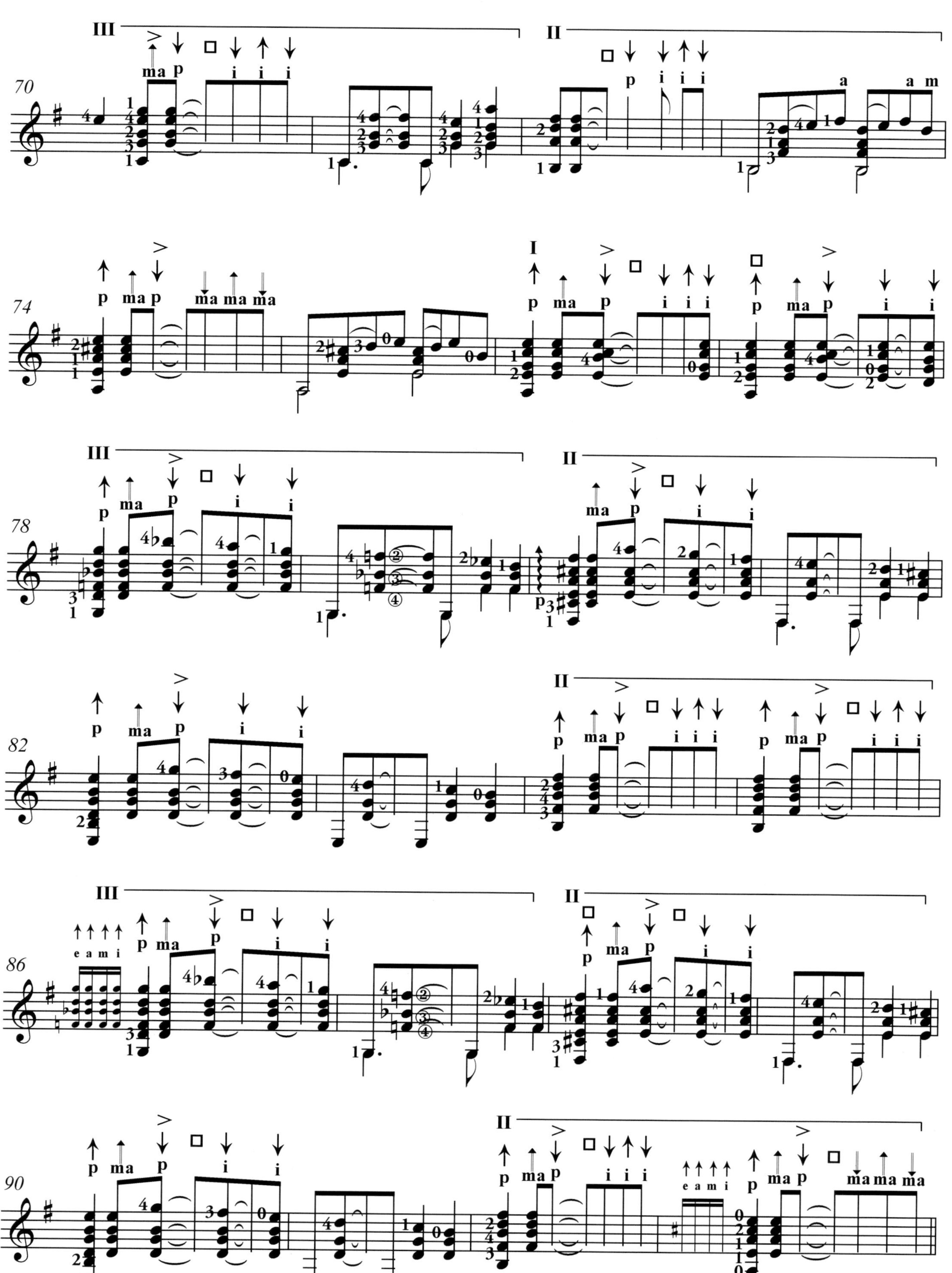
70
III
II
ma p i i i
p i i i a a m
74
I
p ma p ma ma ma
p ma p i i i p ma p i i
78
III
II
p ma p i i
ma p i i
82
II
p ma p i i
p ma p i i i p ma p i i i
86
III
II
e a m i
p ma p i i
p ma p i i
90
II
p ma p i i
p ma p i i i
e a m i
p ma p ma ma ma

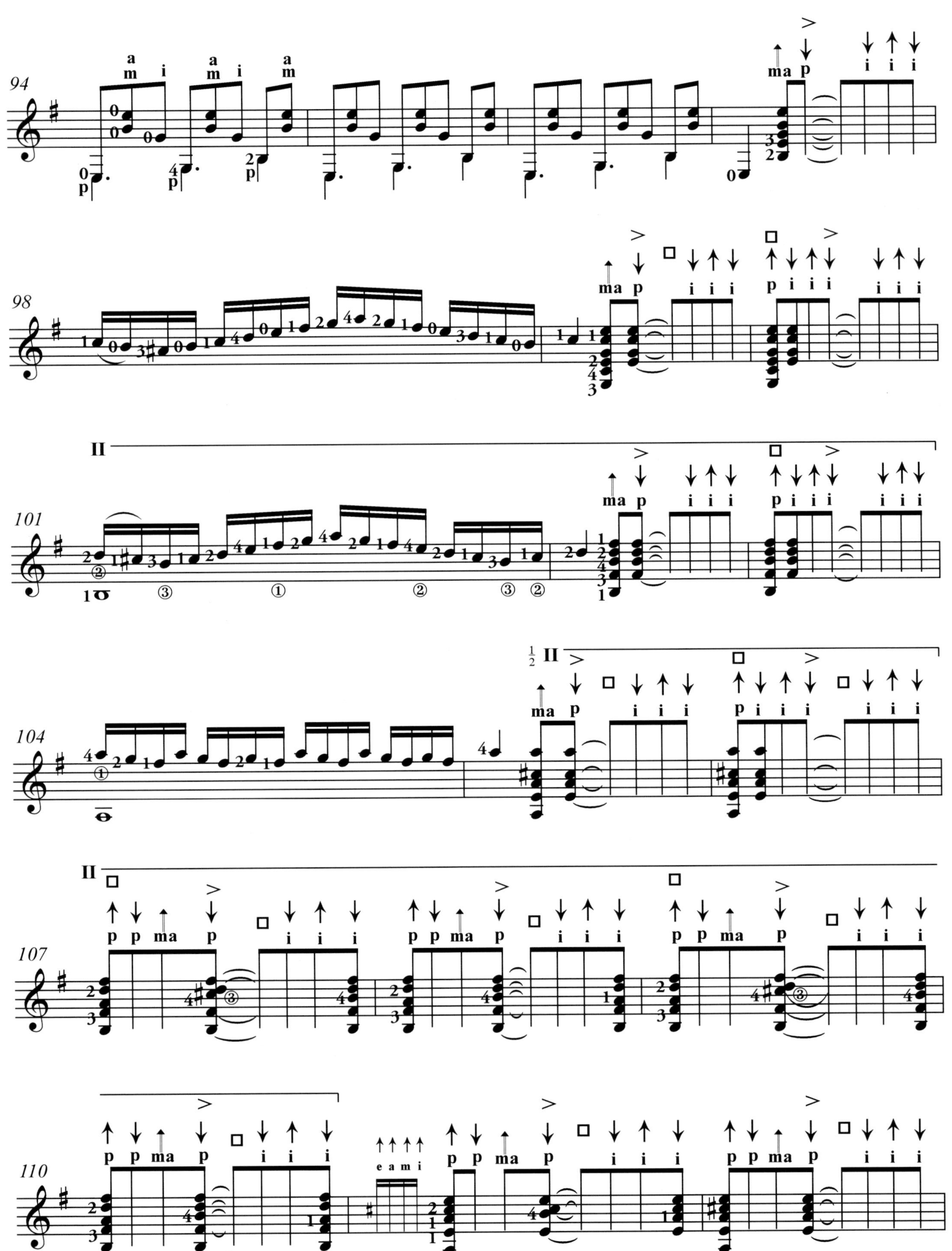
94
a m i a m i a m
ma p i i i
98
ma p i i i p i i i i i i
II
101
ma p i i i p i i i i i i
½ II
104
p i i i p i i i i i i
II
107
p p ma p i i i p p ma p i i i p p ma p i i i
110
p p ma p i i i
e a m i
p p ma p i i i p p ma p i i i

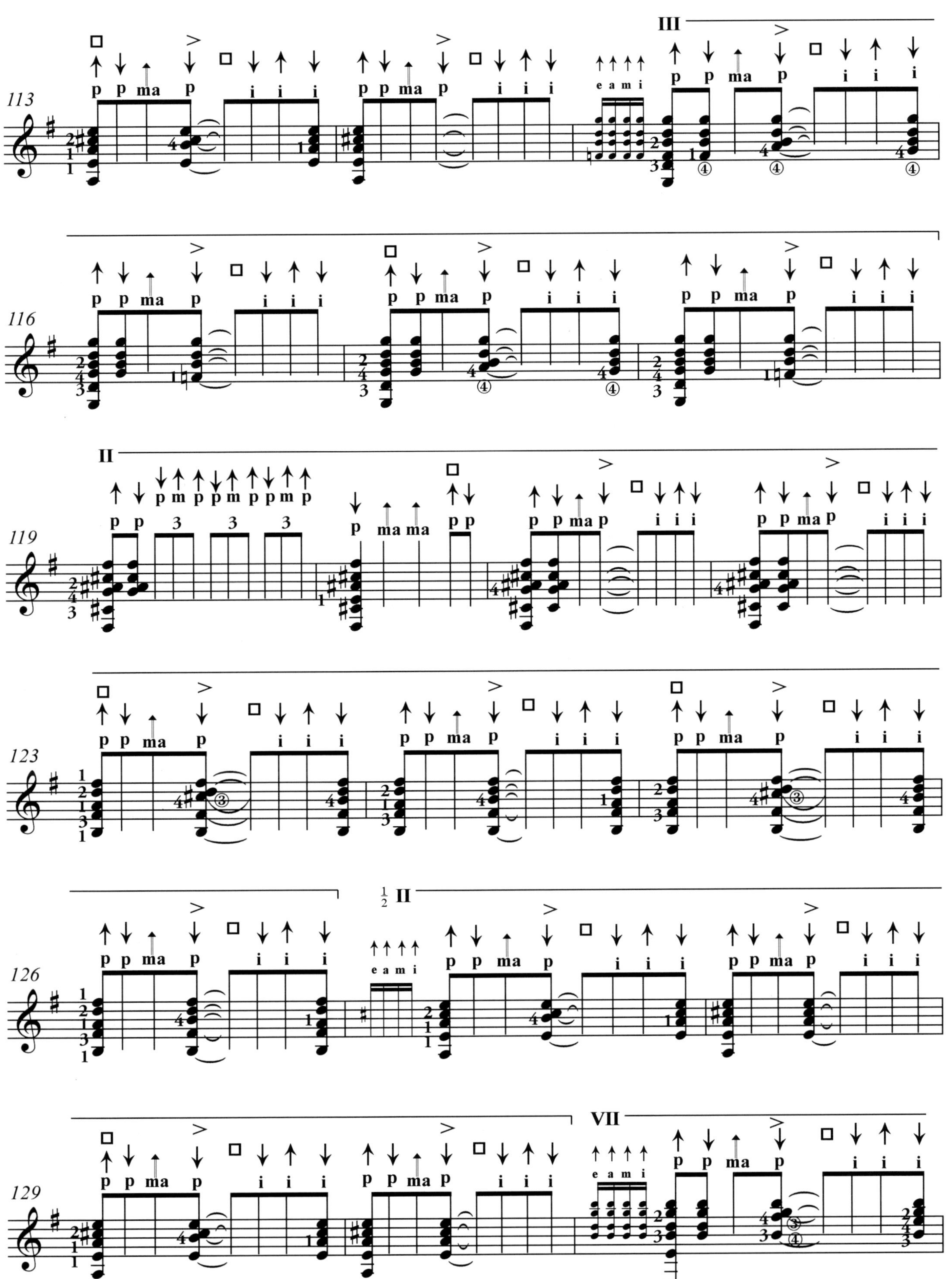
III
113
116
II
119
123
½ II
126
VII
129

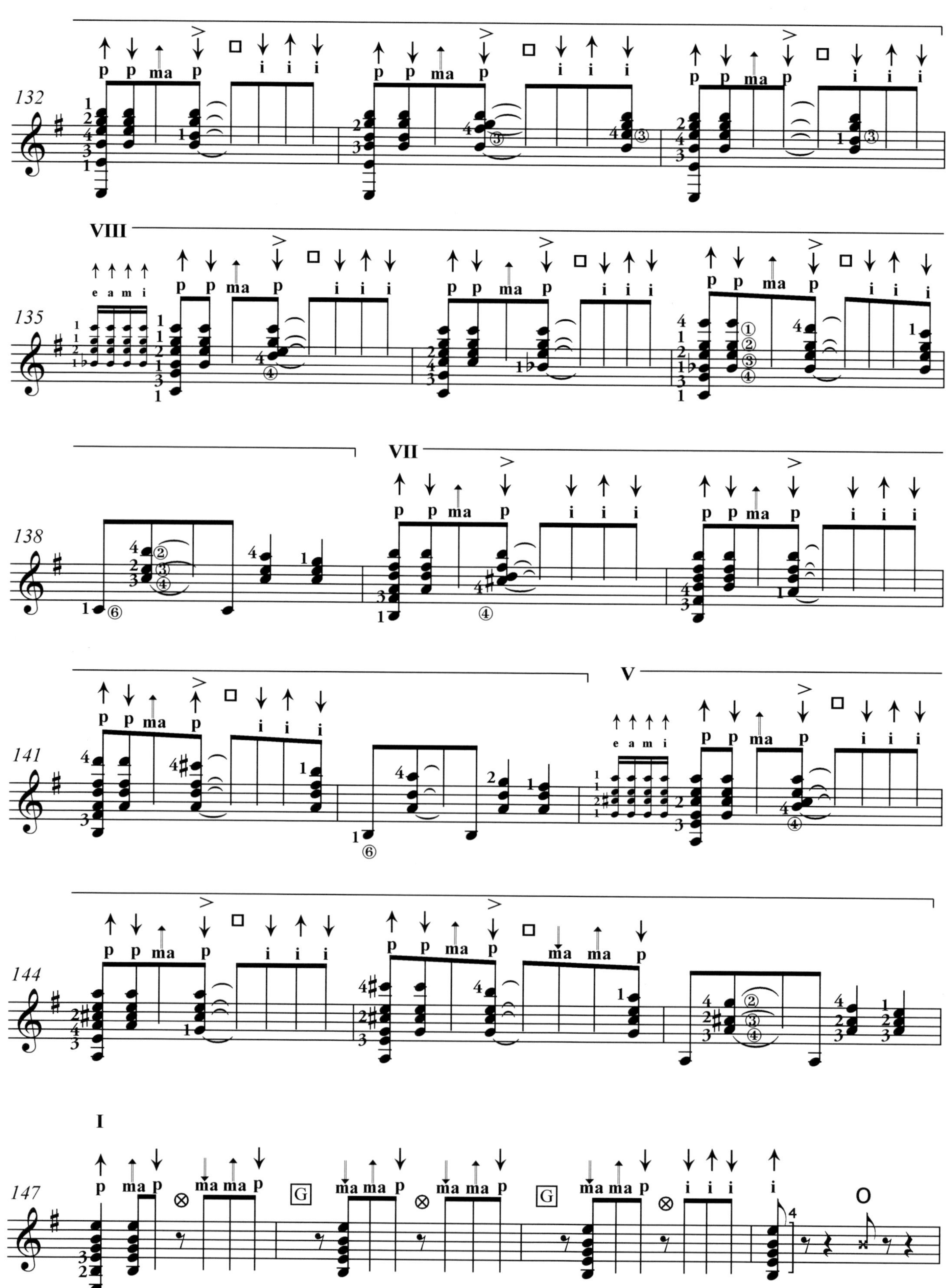
132
p p ma p i i i
VIII
135
e a m i
138
VII
141
V
144
p p ma p ma ma p
I
147
p ma p ma ma p
G
i i i

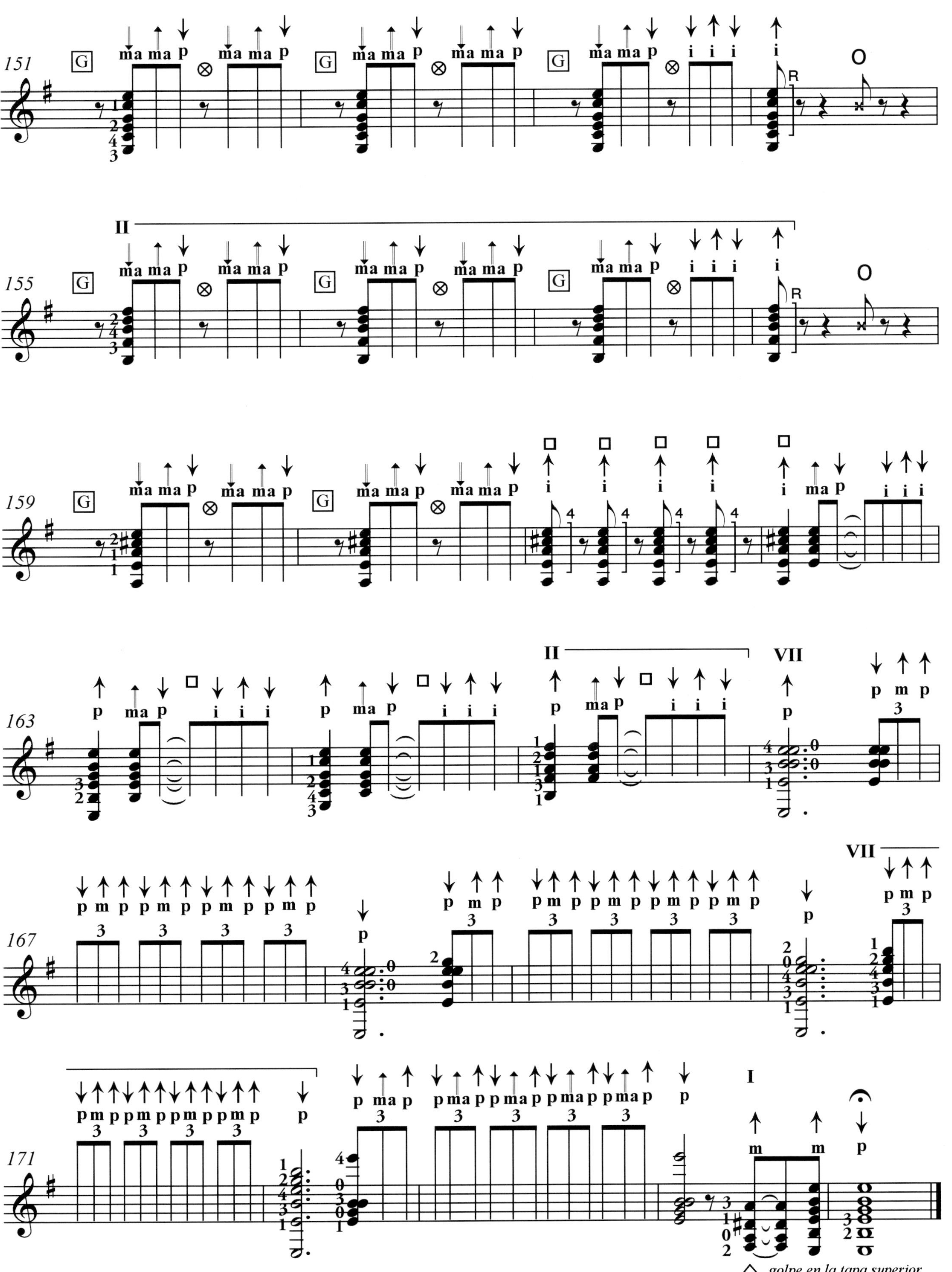
golpe en la tapa superior
golpe above 6th string

Noche en los jardines de Granada

Transcription by
ANGELA CENTOLA

JUAN MARTÍN

13

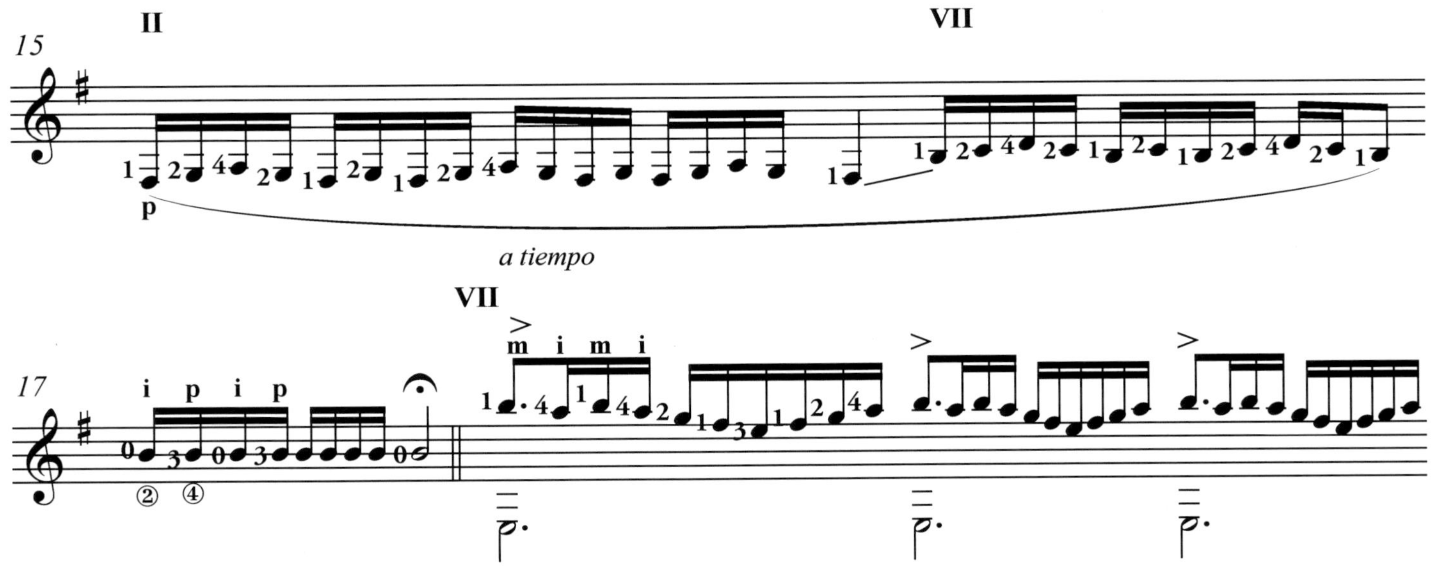
15
II
VII
p
a tiempo
17
VII
i p i p
m i m i

21

23
VII
a
m
i
p

27
II
III
V
III
a
m
i
p

29
II
III V III
V
32
VI VIII VI
V
VI VIII VI III
35
II
III V III
II
tr lento
38
IV
V
IV
V
42
II
I
47
m a m i
I
52
II
VII
i p

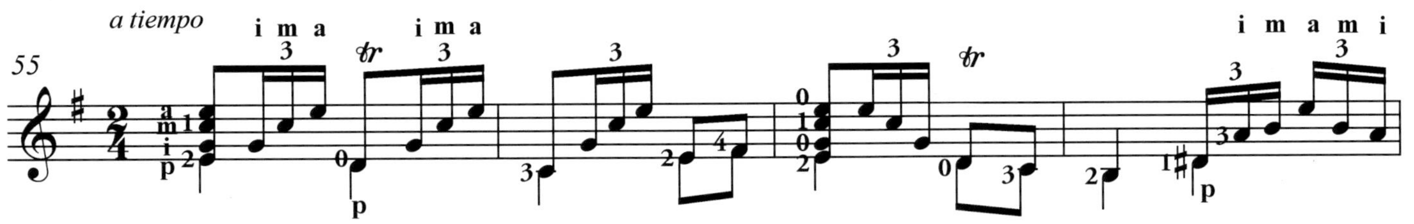
a tiempo
55

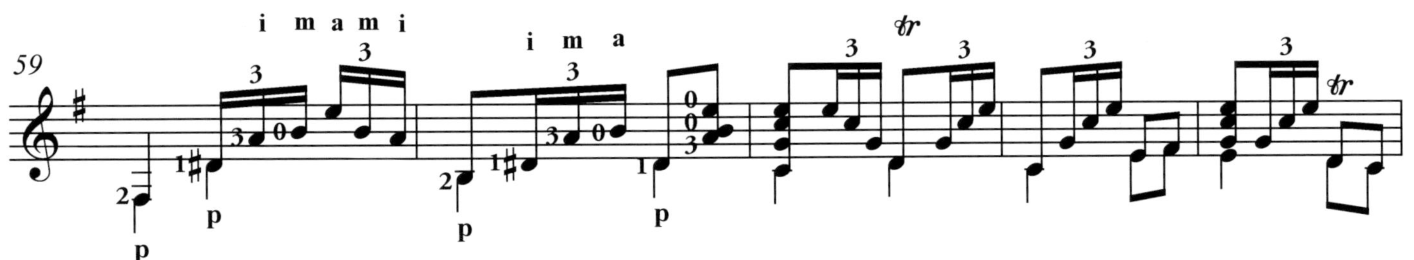
59

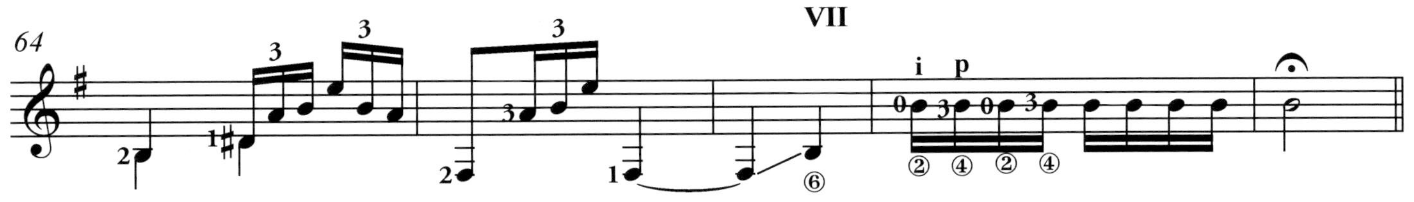
64
VII

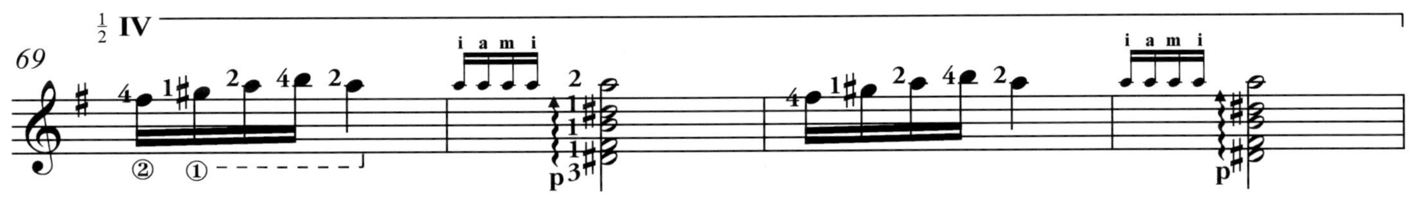
½ IV
69

73

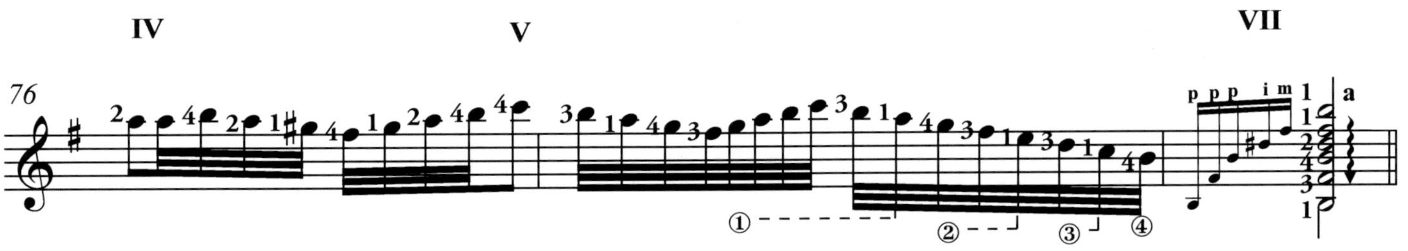
IV
V
VII
76

79
½ VII

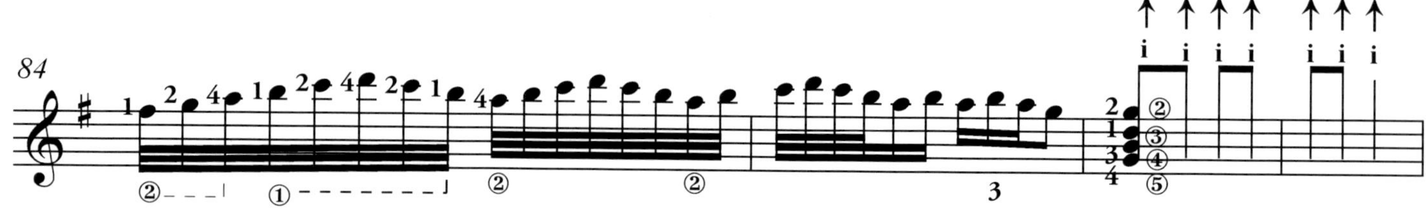
84

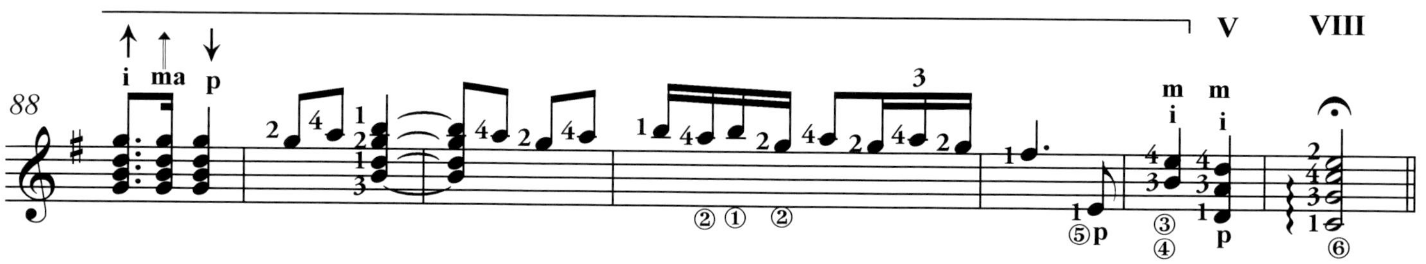
88
V
VIII

95
VIII
VII

98
I

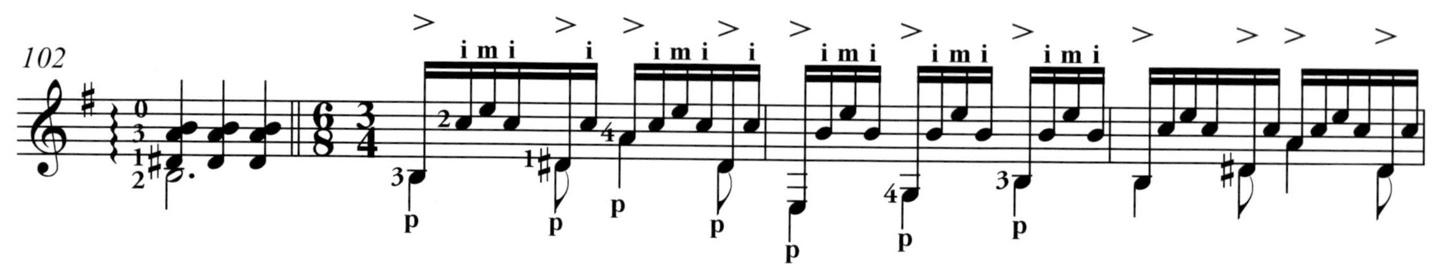
102

III
106
109
112
I
II
117
II
121
124

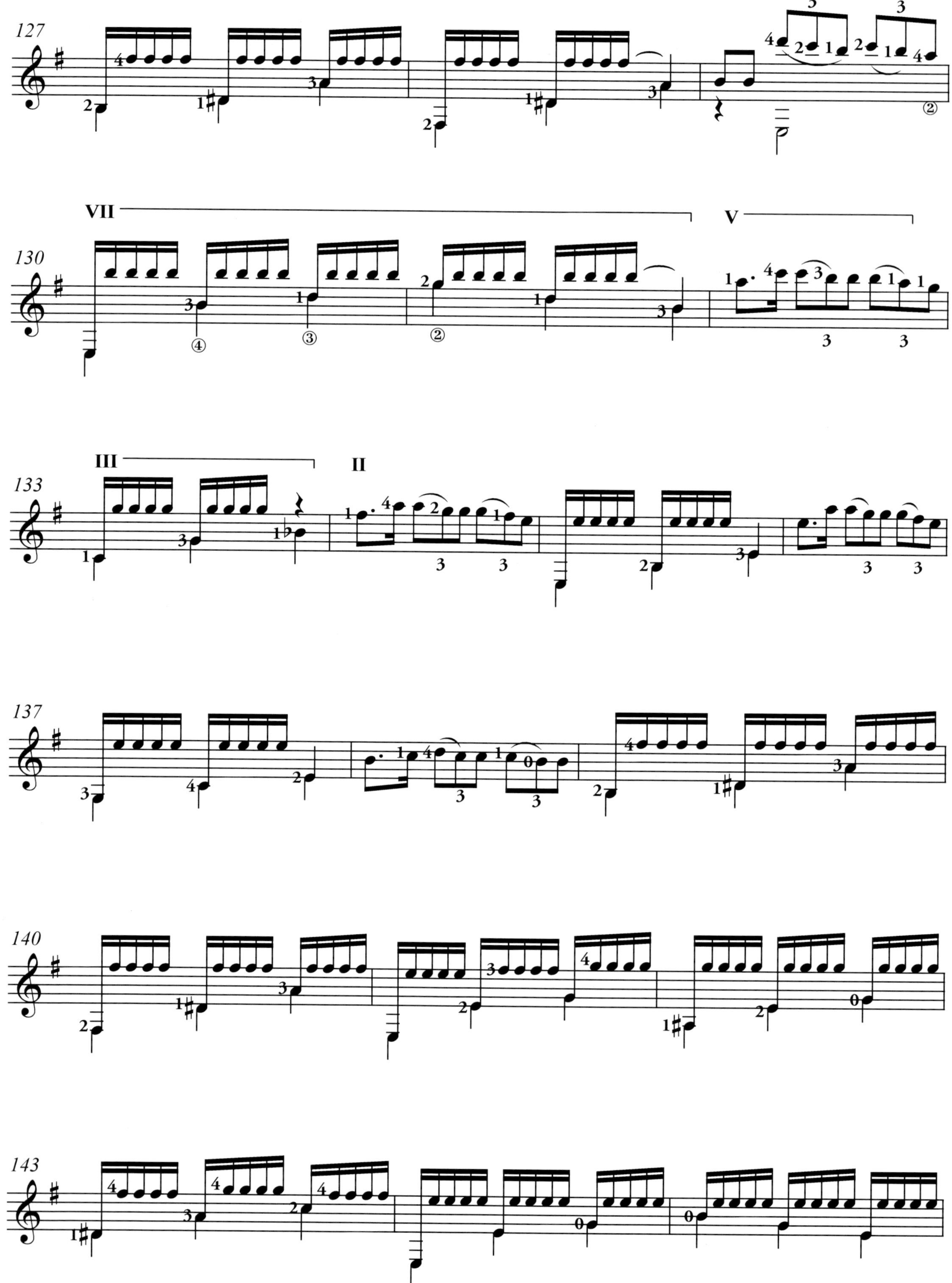

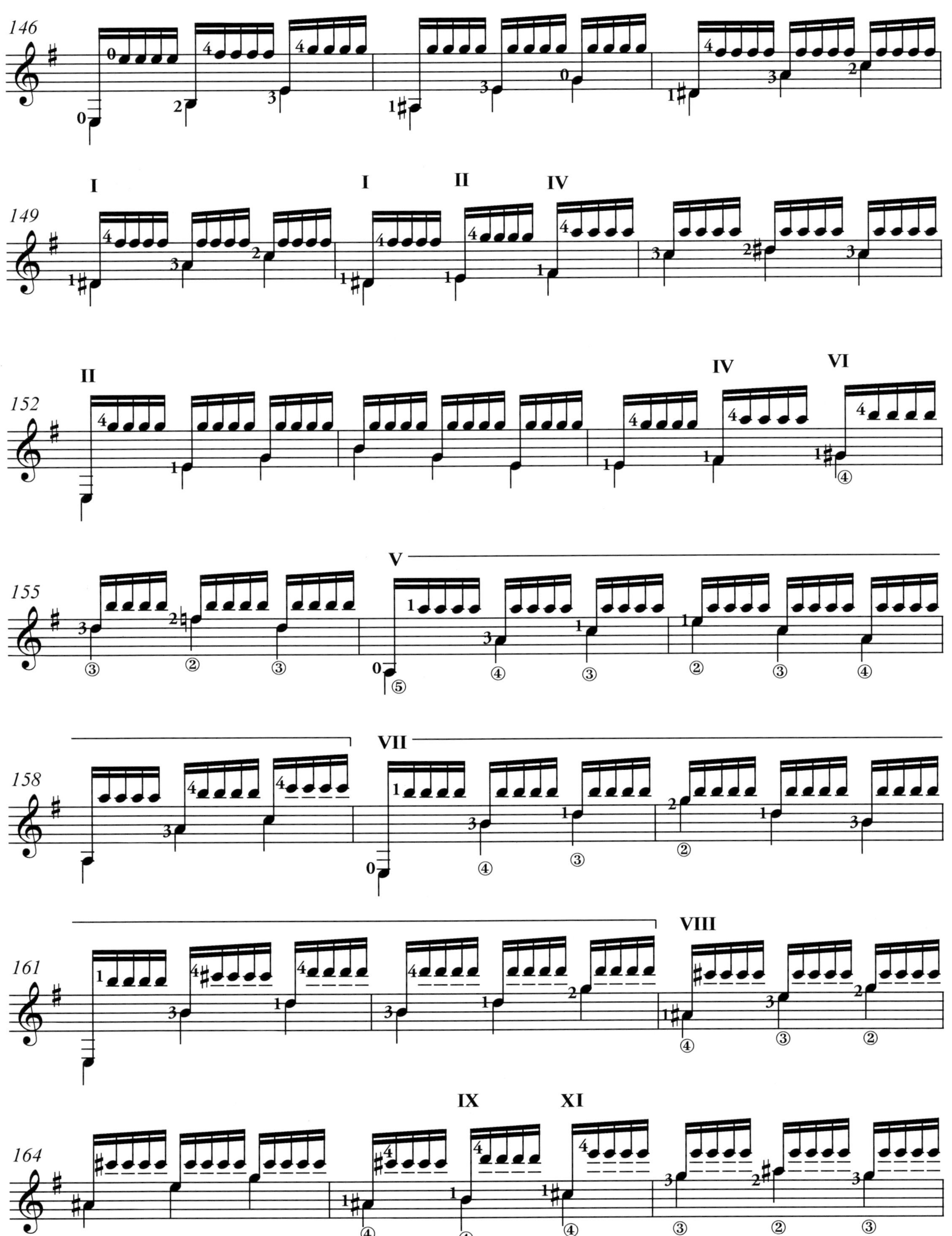
146
149
I I II IV
152
II IV VI
155
V
158
VII
161
VIII
164
IX XI

167
VII
I
170
172
Toque libre
176
VII
179
182
185
II
III
V
III
II

188
III V III V VI VIII VI
191
V VI VIII VI III
193
II III V III II VII
197
VII
199
201
203
Harm. XII

Con Rumbo al Carnaval

Guajiras

Transcription by
ANGELA CENTOLA

6

JUAN MARTÍN

13
½ II
I
16
½ II
I
i m a
19
½ II
22
½ II
i m a m
½ II
25
½ II
i m a m
28
a m i
a m i
II
m a m i

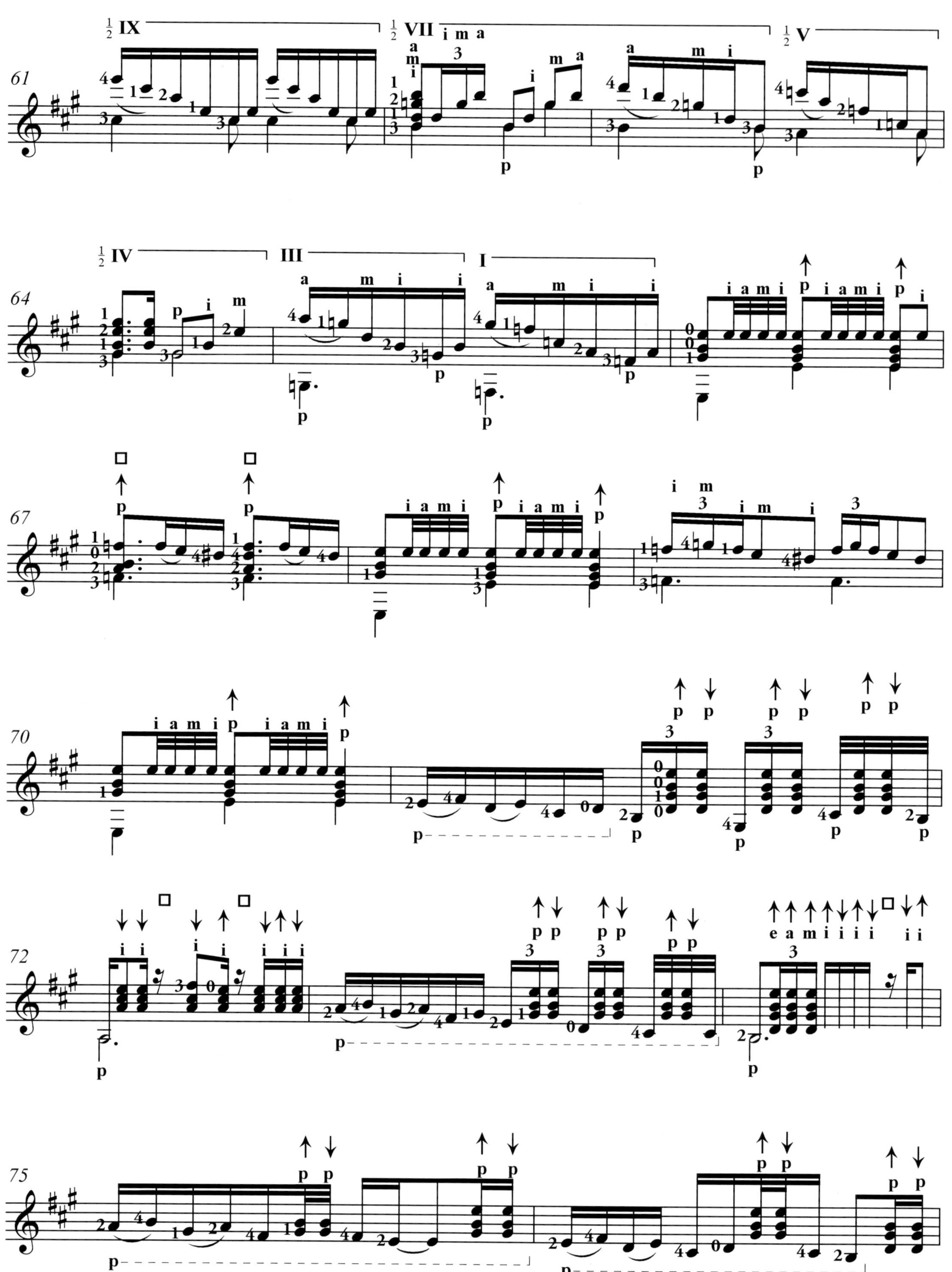

77
i m i m
IV
79
II
i m i
VI
m i m
p p p p p p
½ V
VI
II
82
½ II
p p p p p p
VI
½ V
85
VII
IX
X
88
IX
X
IX
91
X
p i m
IX

93
VII
IV
V
½ IV
½ II
95
97
I
½ II
99
I
101
I
103
IV
V
105
I

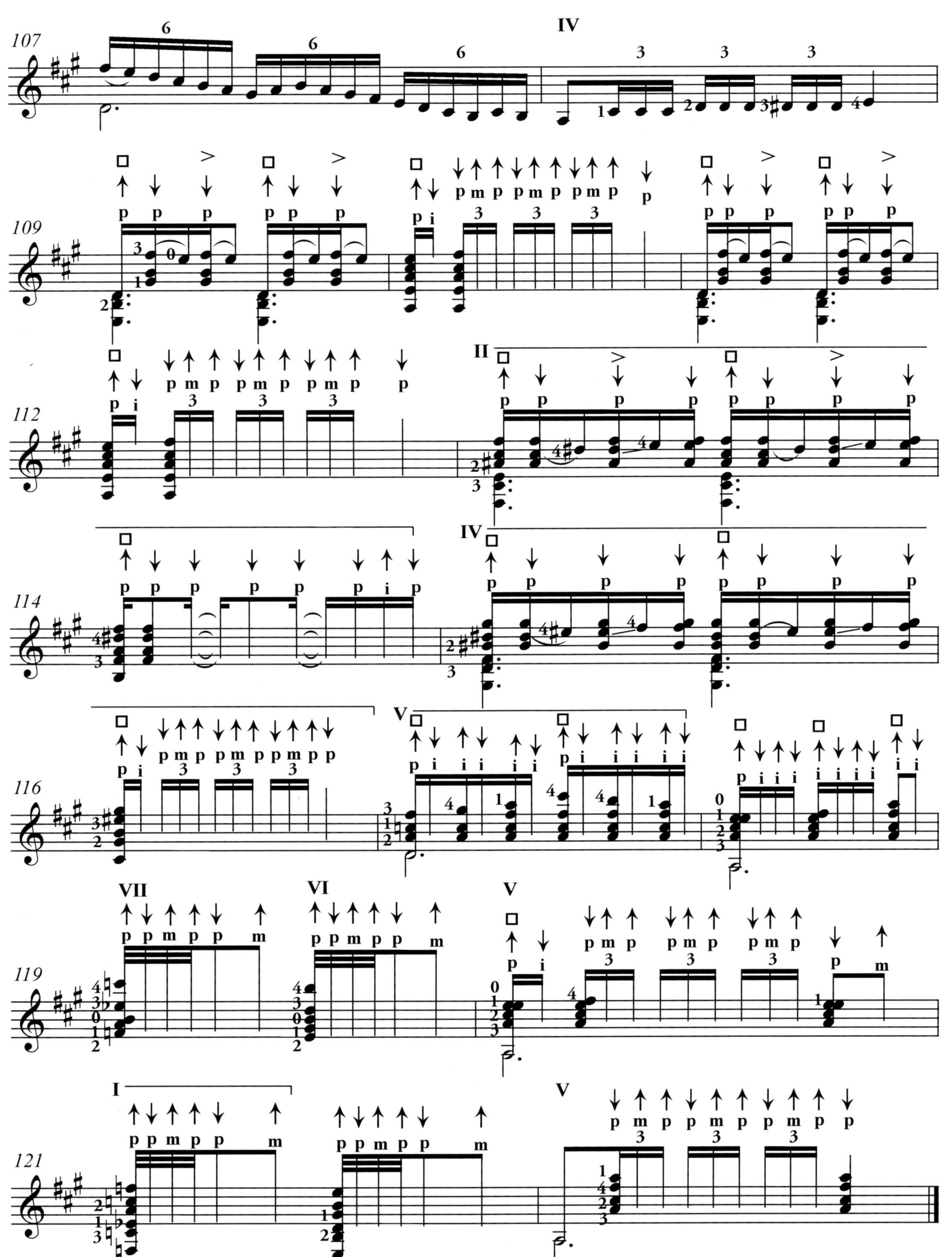
107
IV
109
112
II
114
IV
116
V
119
VII
VI
V
121
I
V

El Tajo de Ronda

Rondeña

Transcription by
ANGELA CENTOLA

7

JUAN MARTÍN

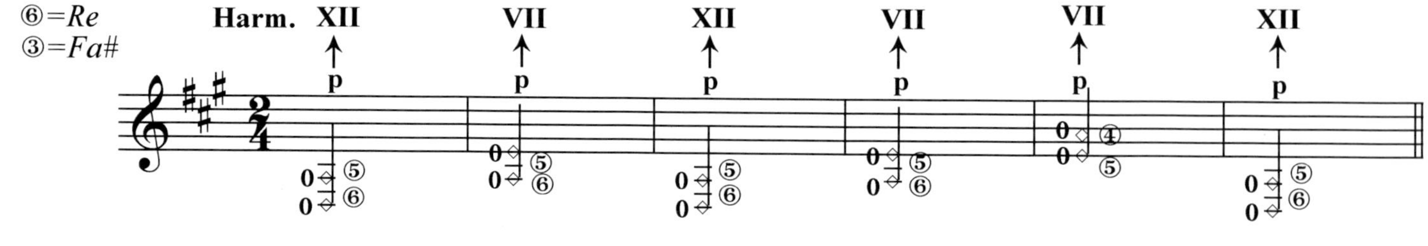

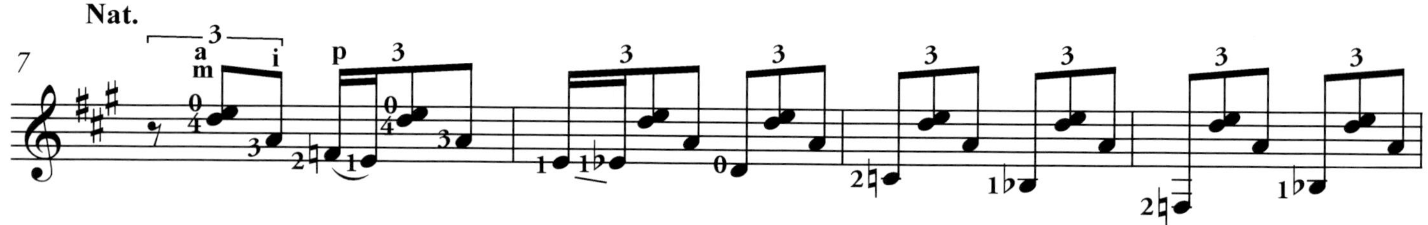

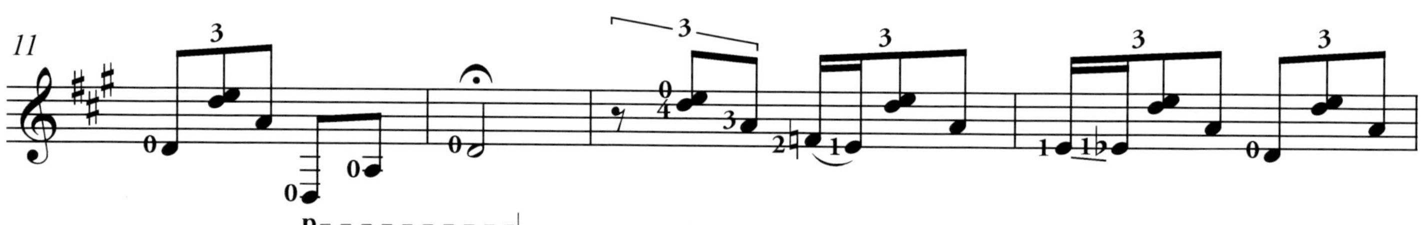

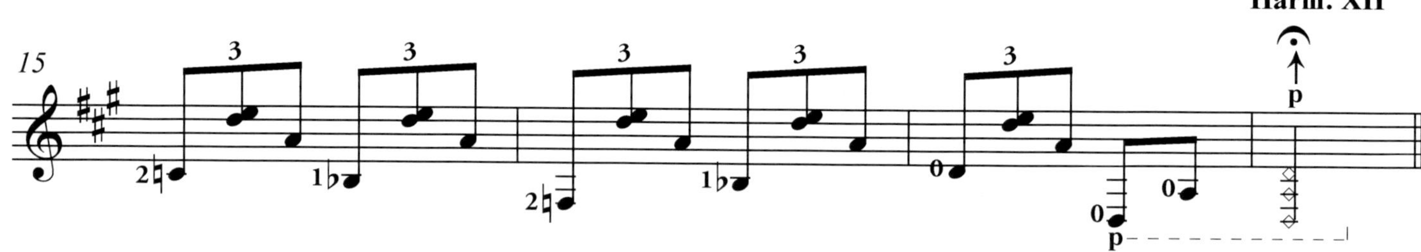

27
V
i m a m
a m i p
31
II
35
39
(p)
42
44
IX
47
XII
XIV

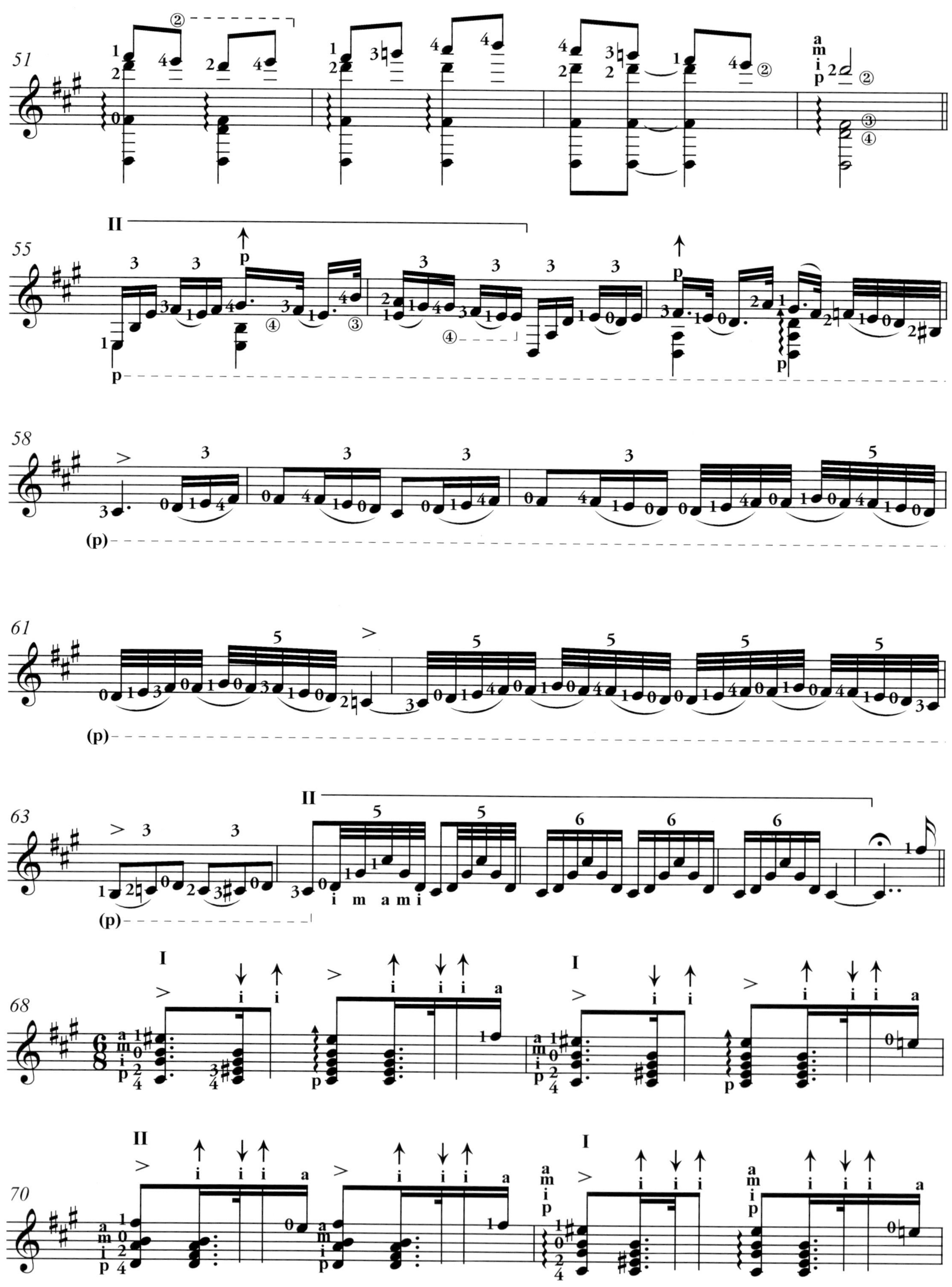
51
55
II
58
(p)
61
(p)
63
(p)
II
i m a m i
68
I
70
II
I

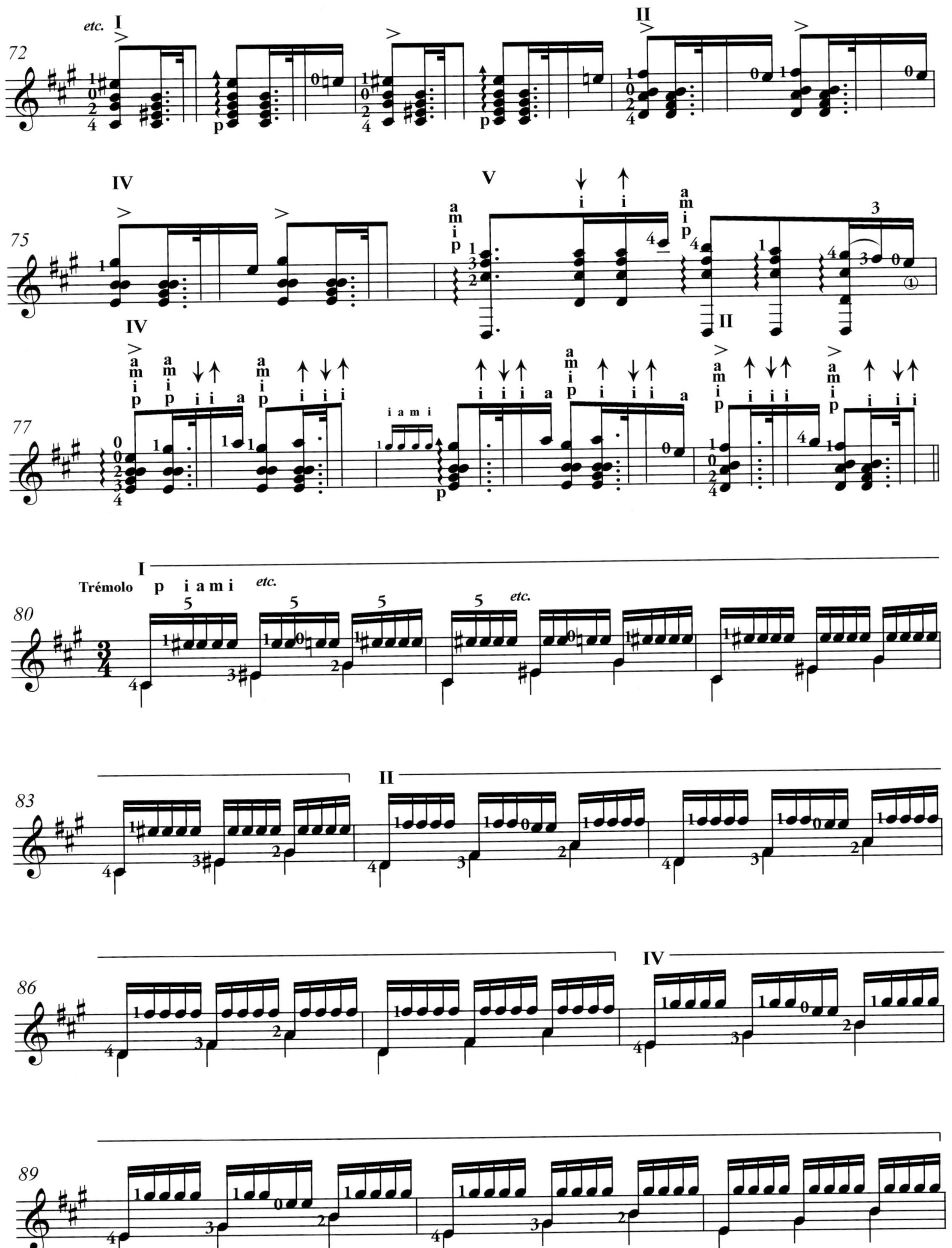
etc.
Trémolo
p i a m i
etc.
etc.

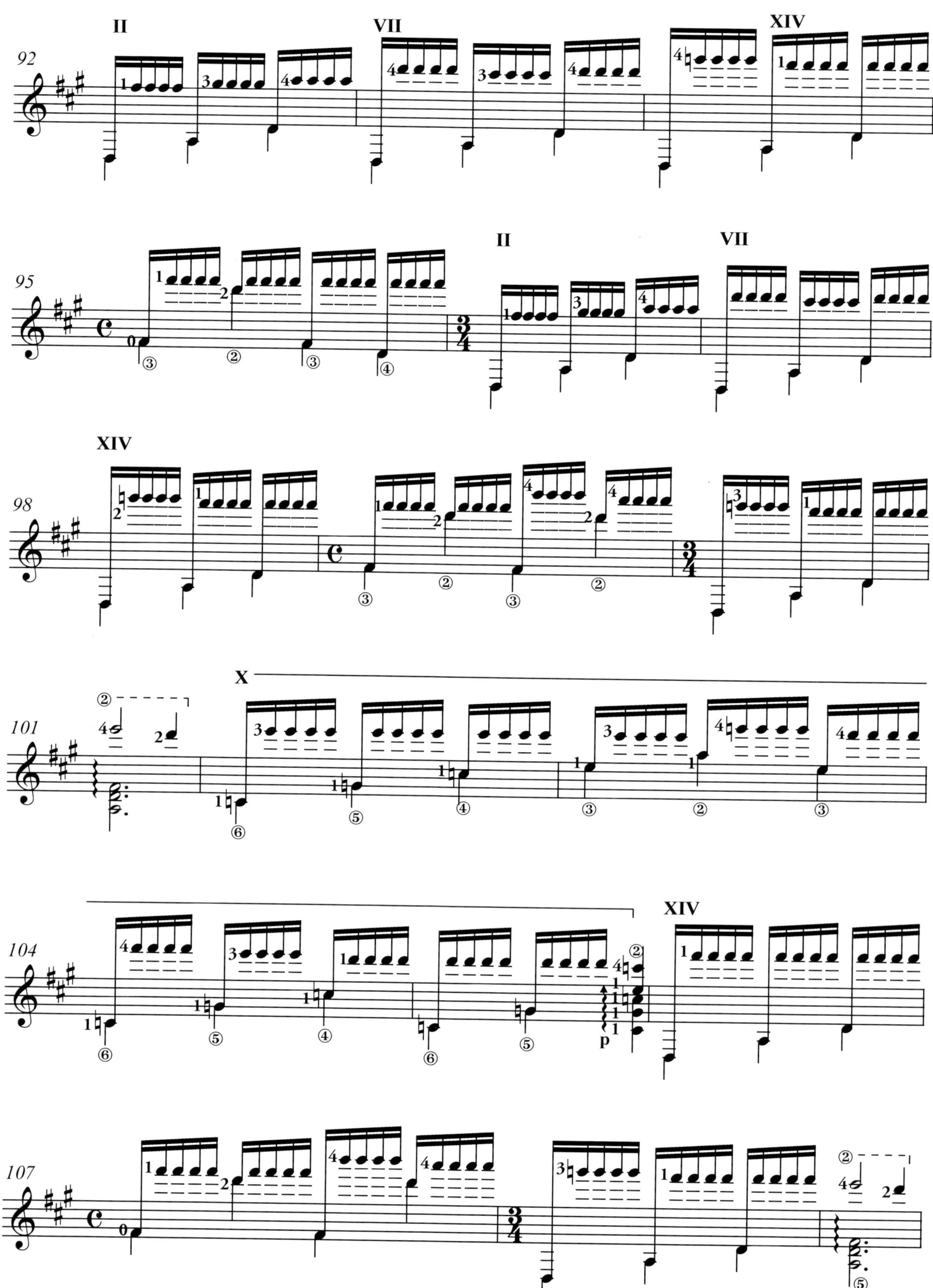
92
II
VII
XIV
95
II
VII
98
XIV
101
X
104
XIV
107

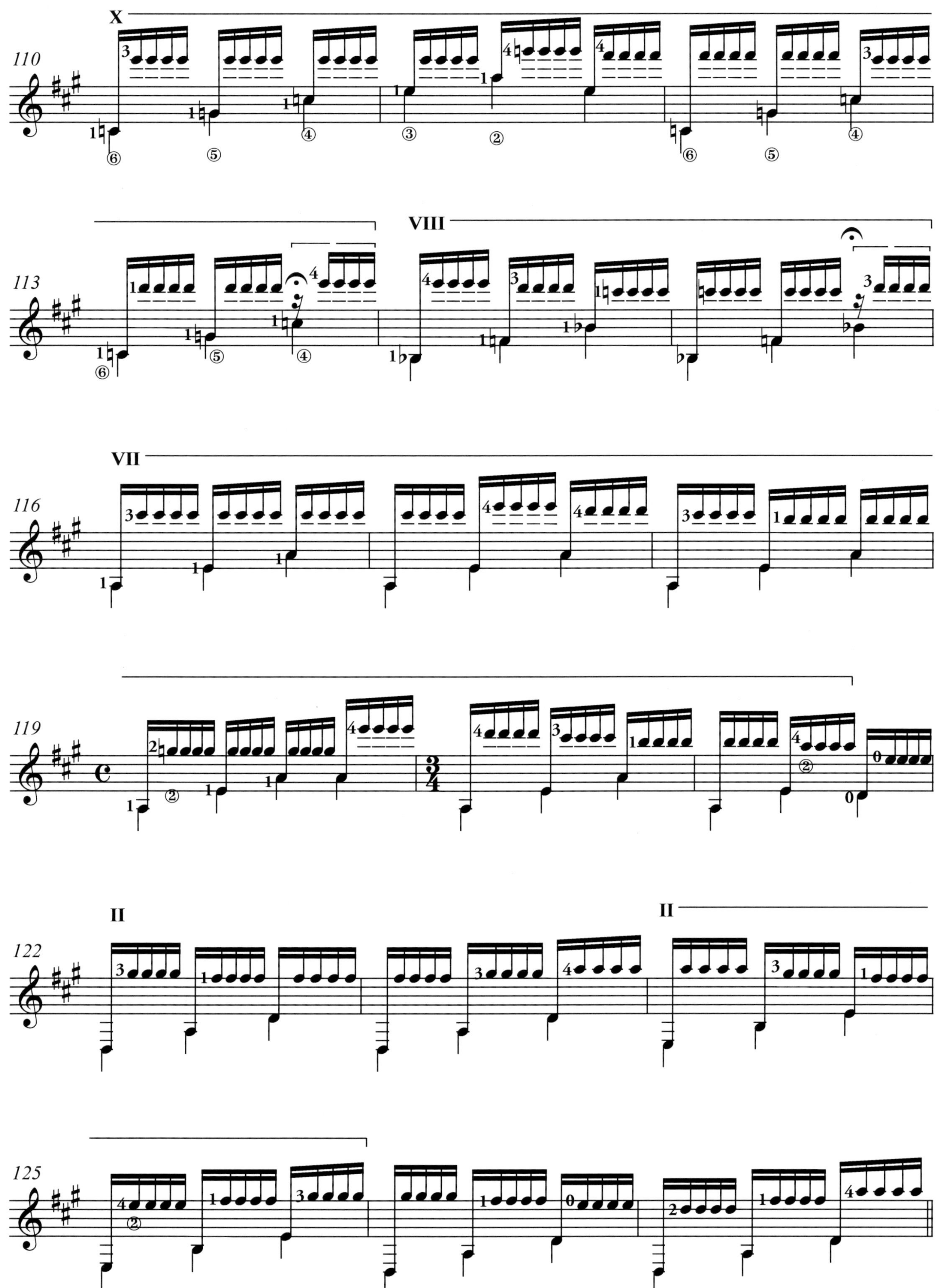
X
VIII
VII
II
II

128
e a m i
130
(p)
½ II
132
i m a m i
6
8
½ X
135
3
4
2
4
138
XIV
142
146
VI
a m i
i m a m i

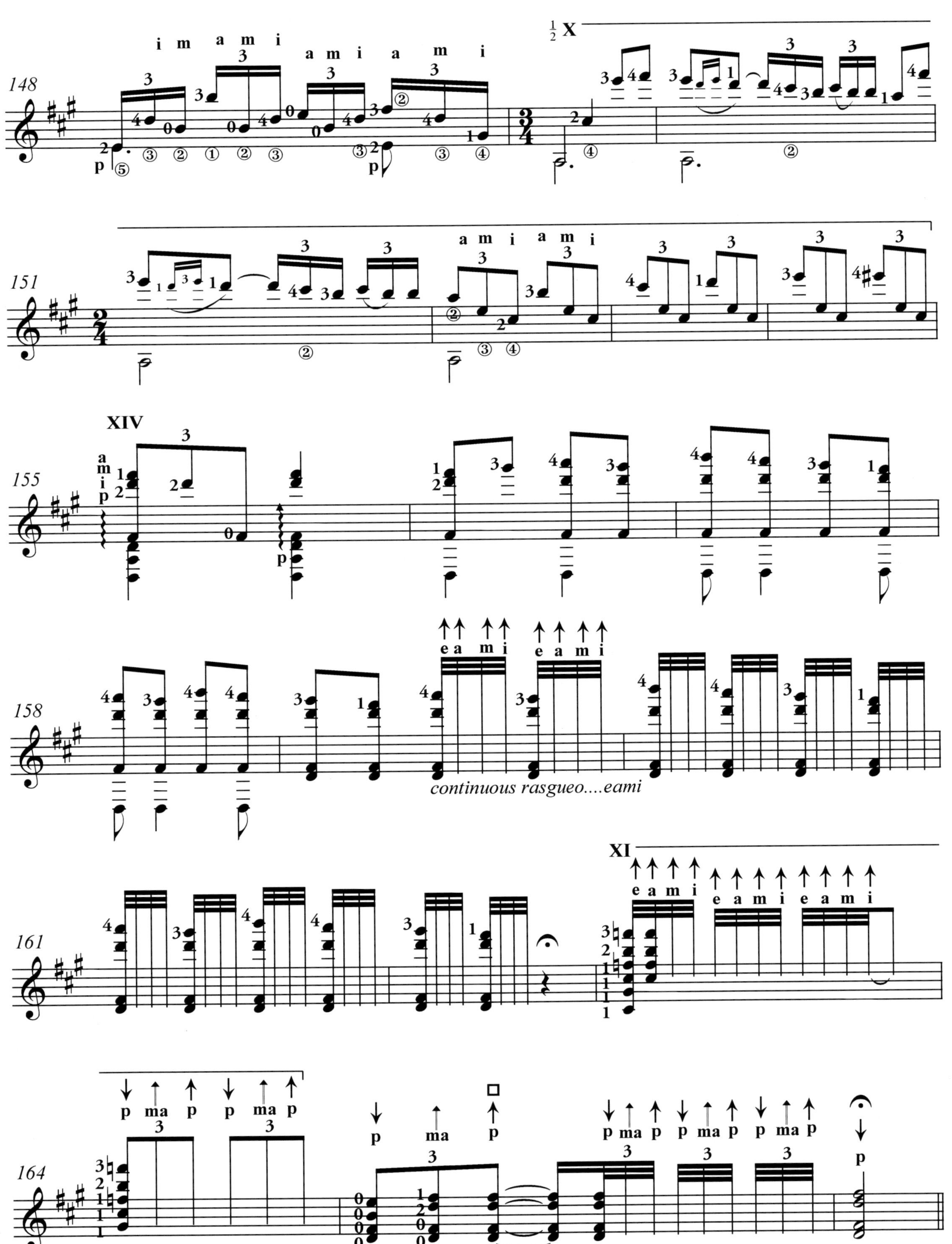
continuous rasgueo....eami

189
193
197
VII
V
II
201
½ II
i m a m i
½ II
IX
205
VII
V
II
209
½ II
i m a m i
½ II
213

Taconeos

Zapateado

Transcription by
ANGELA CENTOLA

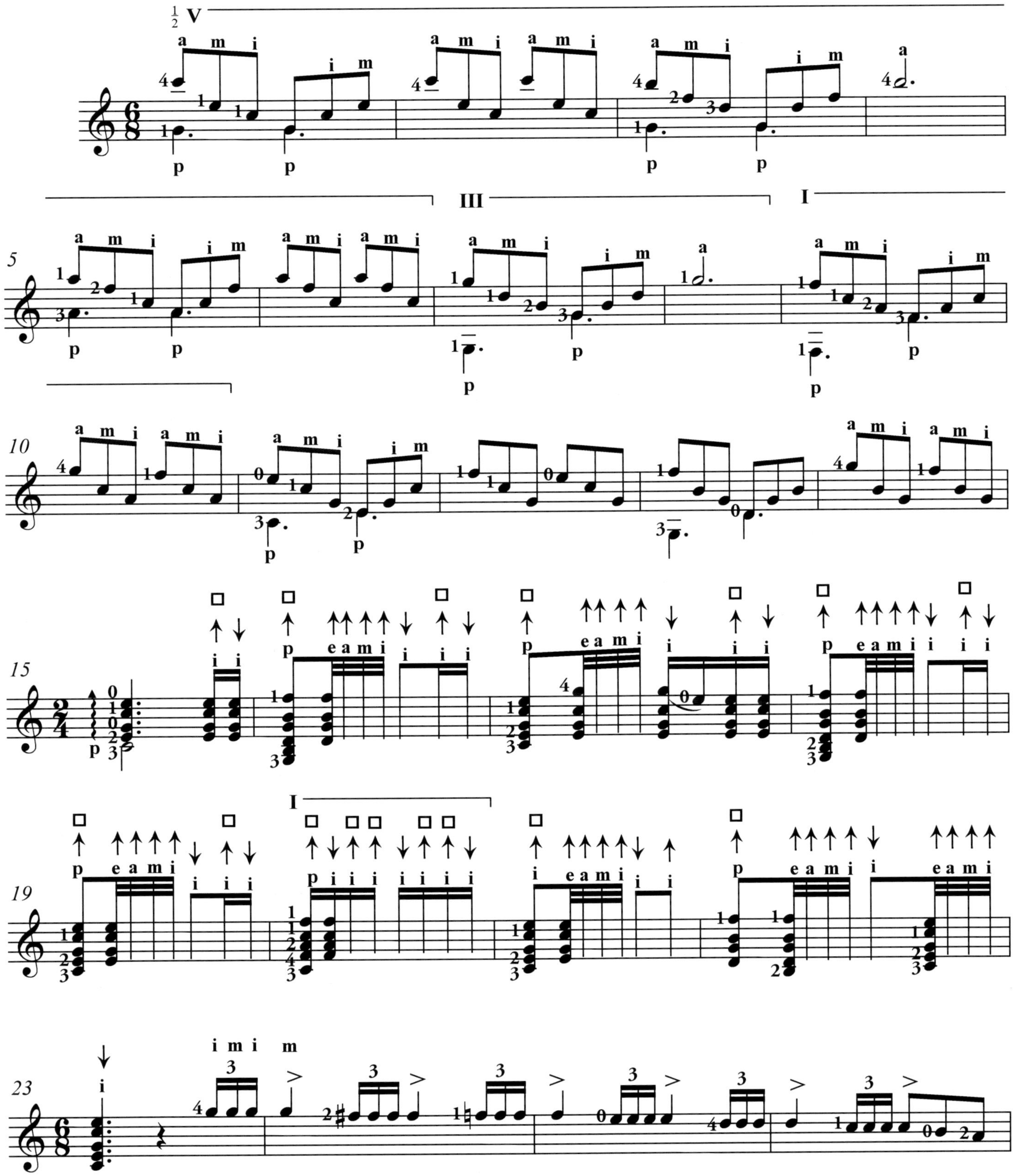

JUAN MARTÍN

27
e a m i i
31
e a m i i
35
39
e a m i
i i i
p e a m i
i i i
p e a m i
i i i
p e a m i
i i i
43
p e a m i
i
m i m
i
47
e a m i i
51
e a m i i

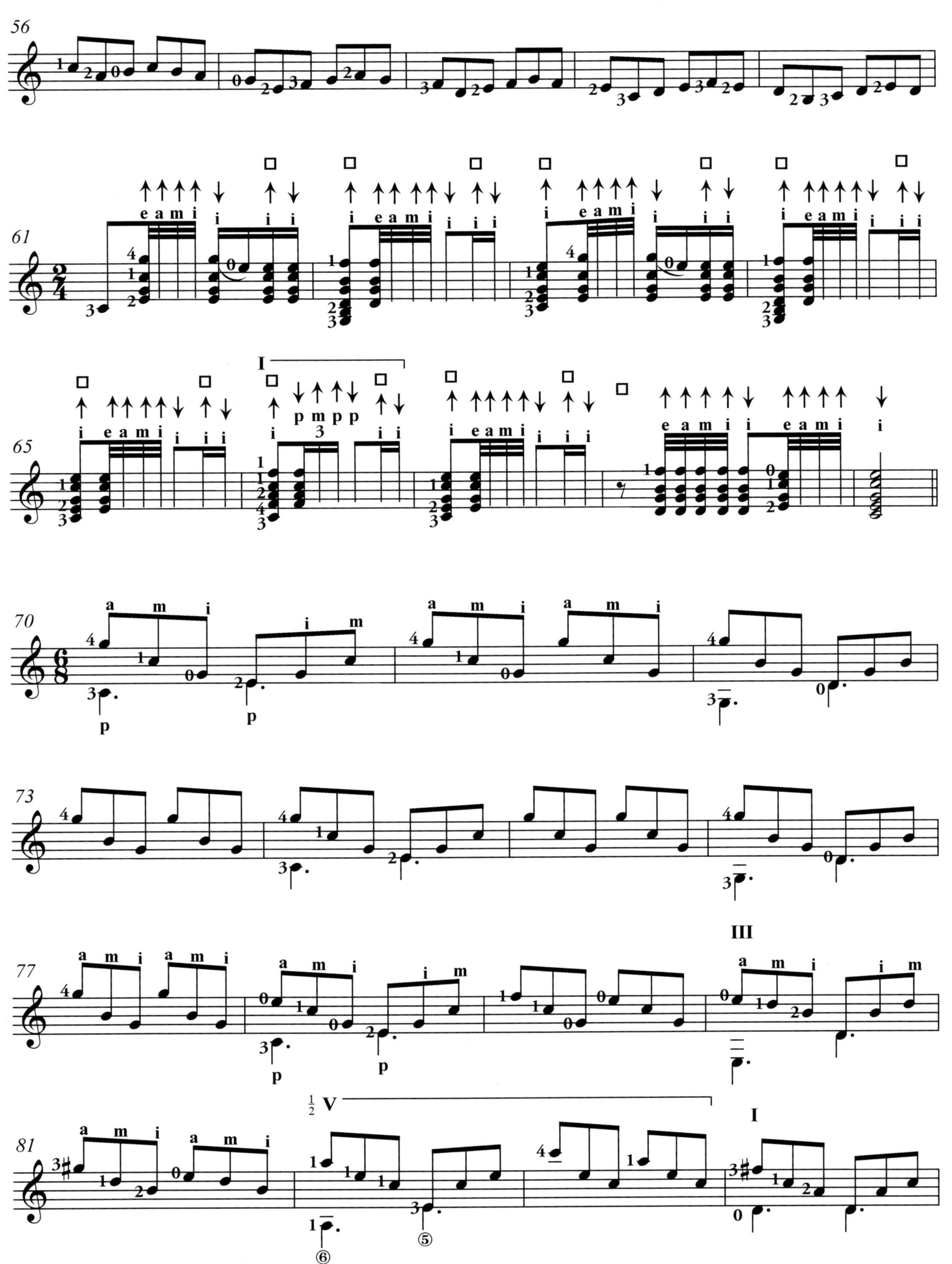

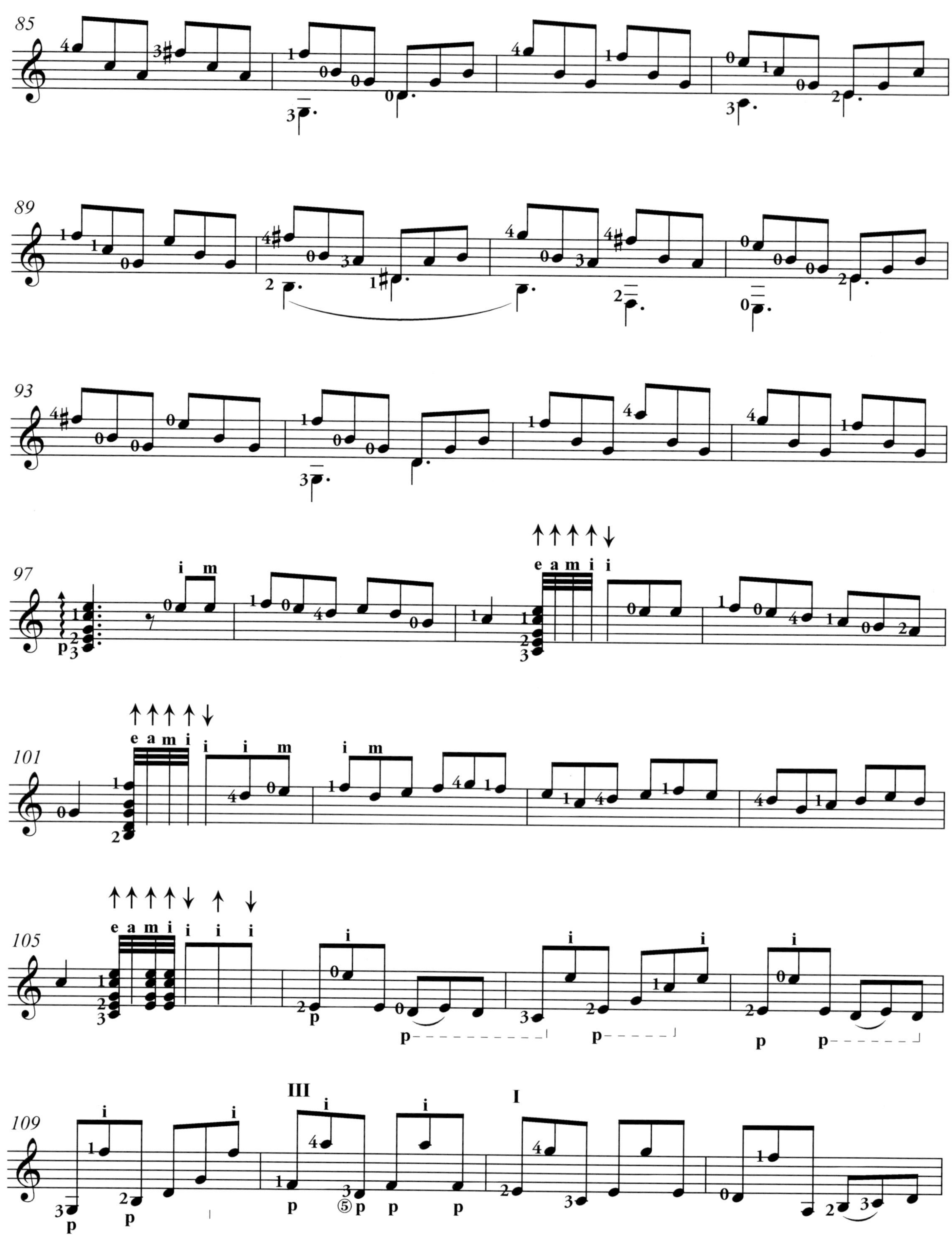
85
89
93
97
101
105
109
III
I

Adagio

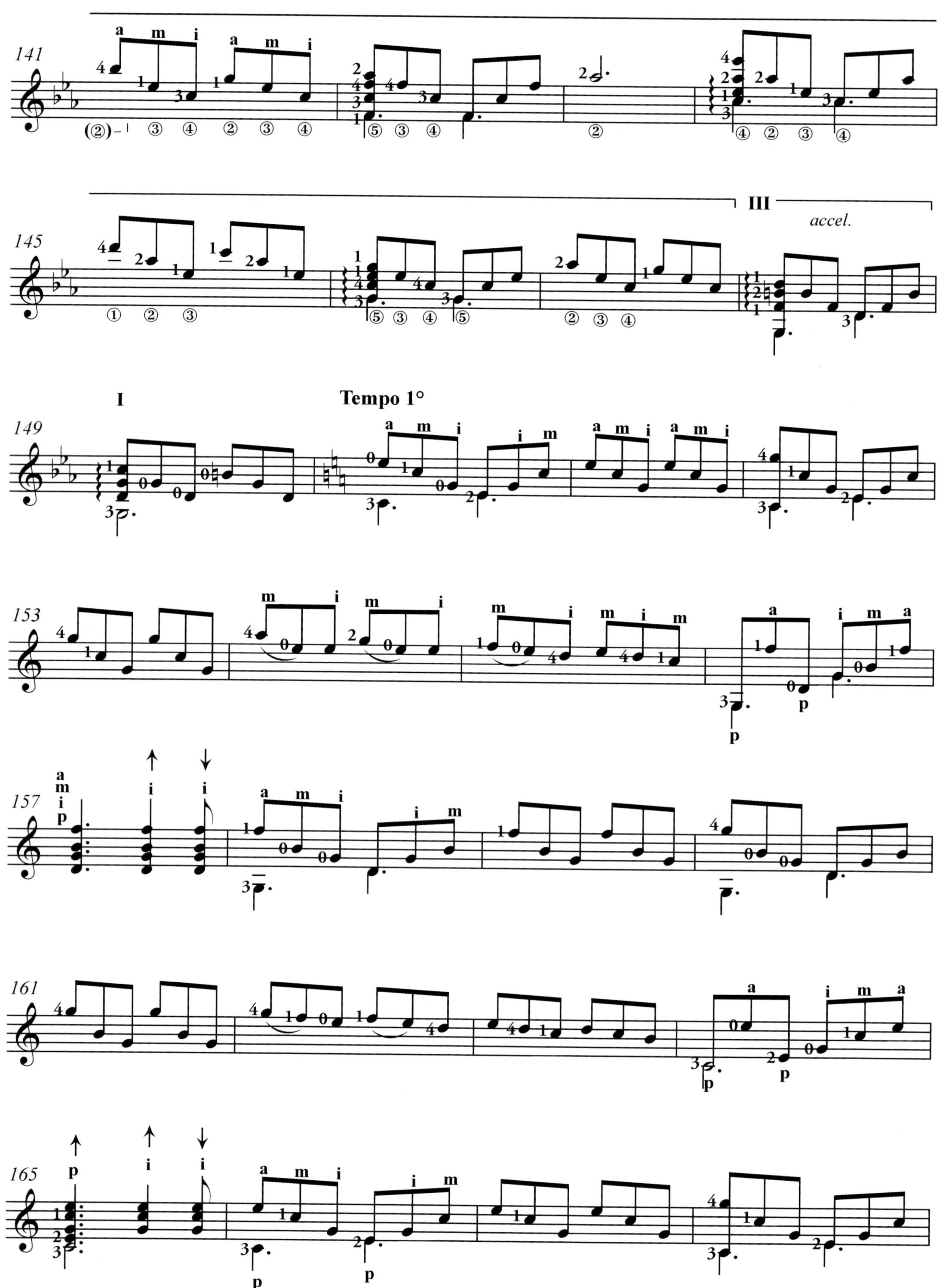
III
accel.
I
Tempo 1°

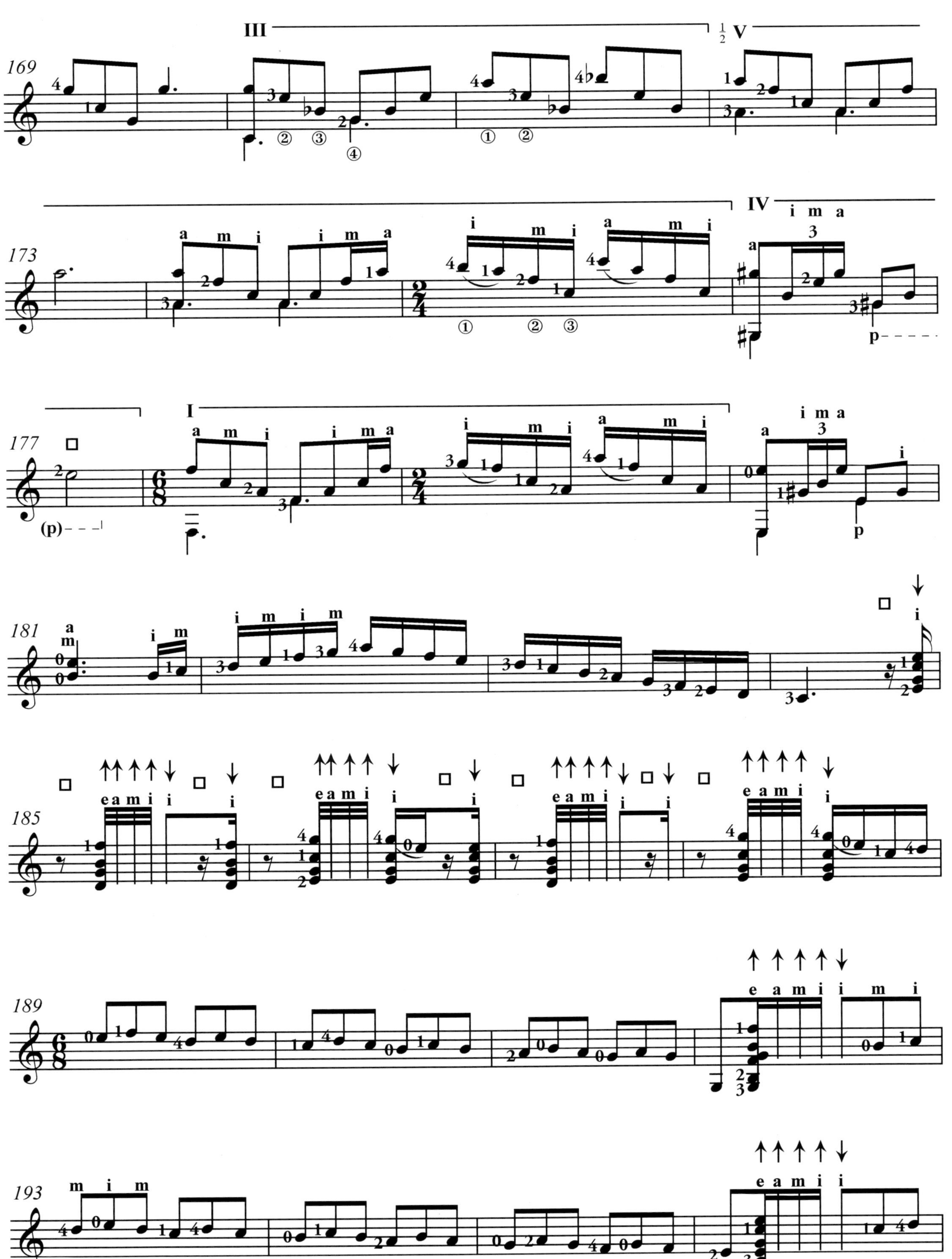

197
I
e a m i i
p
201
e a m i
i
205
e a m i
i
209
e a m i
i
213
m i
217
m i m i m i
221

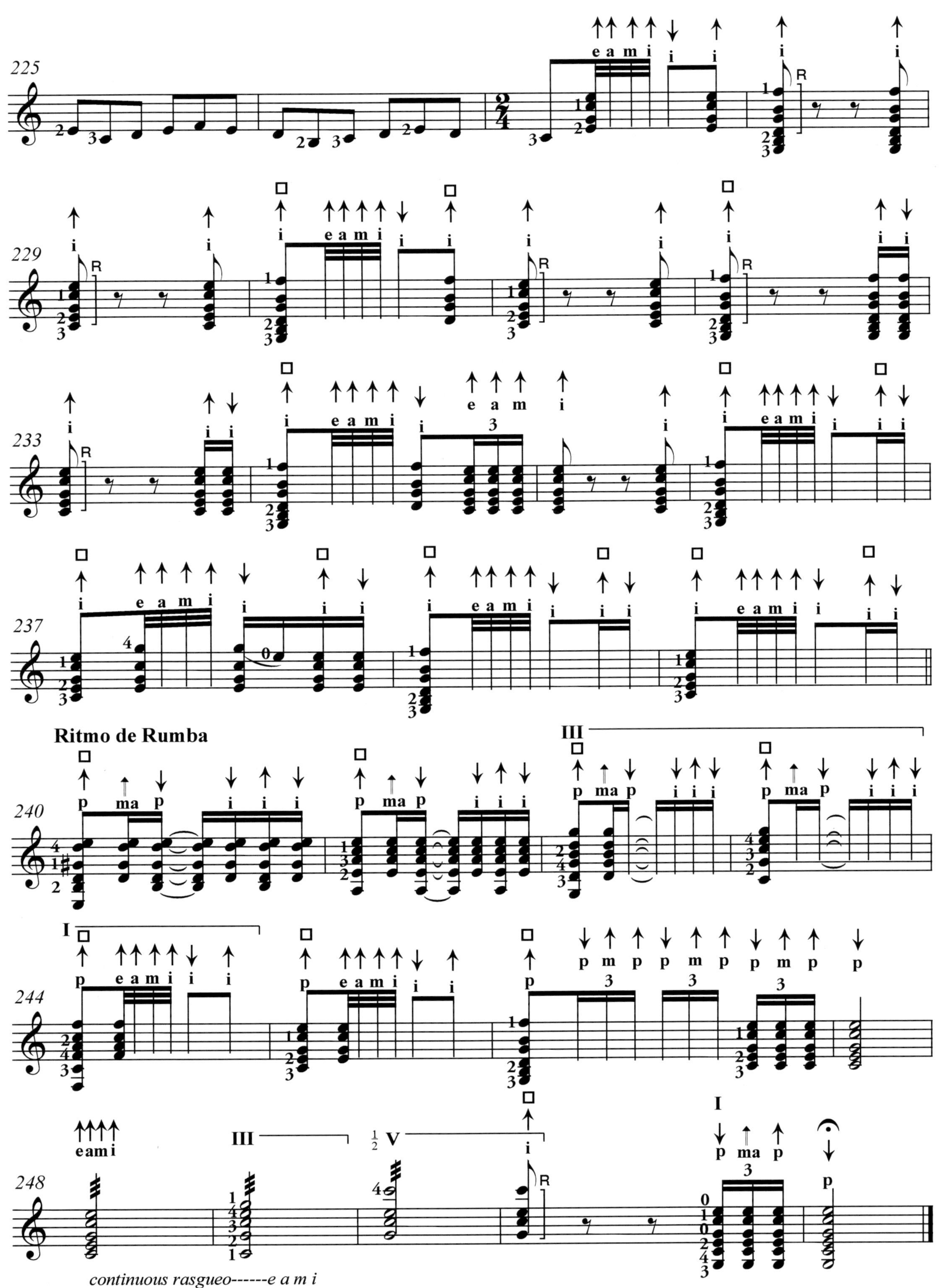
Ritmo de Rumba
continuous rasgueo------e a m i

About the Composer

Juan Martín learned his art in the land of its origin, Andalucía in southern Spain, where he spent his early formative years and where he still retains a house. As a teenager he played in local fiestas, weddings and baptisms, developing his knowledge and skills in the disciplines of the purest traditions of flamenco. At the age of 17, already playing professionally, he performed in the film *Donde tu estés*, filmed in the Málaga region, and at the age of 18 he went to Madrid, where he gained wide experience with many leading singers, players and dancers. He was greatly influenced by the example and encouragement of the legendary guitarist Niño Ricardo and Juan was a regular visitor at the home of Paco de Lucía in Madrid.

These early years playing in the heartland of flamenco provided the basis for his subsequent career as a solo performer and leader of his own dance companies, a challenging vocation which has brought him international acclaim as an innovative concert performer, broadcaster and recording artist.

For two years running he was voted into the magazine *Guitar Player*'s poll-winners in the flamenco section, and he was invited to perform at Picasso's 90th birthday celebration. He has performed at major arts festivals including the Montreux Jazz Festival with Miles Davis and Herbie Hancock, the First World Guitar Congress in the USA, Istanbul, Hong Kong, Shanghai, The London Guitar Summit and many more. In Andalucía he was featured in flamenco festivals in Ojén, Málaga and Cádiz provinces, sharing the bill with Paco Cepero, Paco del Gastor, Vicente Amigo, El Pele, El Cabrero, Juanito Villar, La Macanita and Parilla de Jerez, Amparo Heredia 'La Repompilla' and dancer David Morales.

His interest in the Moorish roots of flamenco led him to record *Música Alhambra,* rediscovering Andalusí and Sephardic music from the 12th and 13th centuries. "Martín spans the centuries with a mixture of the dazzling and the profound", commented Britain's *Observer* newspaper. More recent CDs have included *La Guitarra – Mi Vida* (2015) with Chaparro de Málaga, *Guitar Maestro*, a collection of his recordings including pieces with the Royal Philharmonic Orchestra from his album *Serenade*, *The Early Years*, pieces recorded with the major labels Decca and EMI and the great gypsy singer Rafael Romero 'El Gallina', *El Alquimista* recorded in Andalucía, *Riquezas* with flamenco singer Antonio Aparecida, the Latin-influenced *Camino Latino* with Airto Moreira and Flora Purim, a 2 CD live recording of a concert performance by his dance company *Live en Directo* and *El Embrujo de la Guitarra*, a 3 CD Spanish compilation with tracks of his amongst others by Paco de Lucía and Manolo Sanlucar.

These and his many other recordings are available on all major download and streaming services. His tours around the world have included China, Australia, Iran, the USA, Canada and Europe including a 22-date UK tour with the number one Spanish dancer, Eva La Yerbabuena.

His compositions bring together a distillation of his extensive knowledge of traditional flamenco styles with his own inventive interpretations of the music. They show his mastery of the wide range of flamenco palos (rhythmic forms) which originate from the different regions of Andalucía and the very distinctive *propio sello* (his own stamp and creativity) and uncompromisingly flamenco spirit, often illuminated by a strong visual sense of places, people and paintings, that characterize the remarkable range and depth of his artistry today. Especially characteristic of his playing are an unusually profound sensitivity to the beauties of sound of which the guitar is capable and a powerful rhythmic impetus.

These qualities have led to invitations to give solo recitals in some of the finest concert halls in the world from London's Wigmore and Queen Elizabeth Halls to the Herbst in San Francisco, Carnegie and Merkin in New York, Zurich's Tonhalle, Alte Oper in Frankfurt, Amsterdam's Concertgebouw, the Music Conservatoire in Sydney, City Hall Hong Kong to Casa de Pilatos in Seville. Reviewers have compared his compositions to those of the great Spanish composers, Tárrega and Turina.

A passionate desire to communicate the mysteries of flamenco to a wider audience of guitarists led to the publication in 1978, of Juan Martín's enduringly best-selling Guitar Method, *El Arte Flamenco de la Guitarra*, with CD. His 1991 video series, *La Guitarra Flamenca*, is now re-released by Faber as a book with 2 DVDs. Two volumes of progressively graded solos, each with online video and audio, *Solos Flamencos,* as well as two further books with online video, *Essential Flamenco*, are published by Mel Bay Publications and have become best-sellers.

Since 2011 he has held an annual guitar course in Ronda, Andalucía and this, along with his demanding schedule, emphasizes Juan's deep loyalty to the roots of his art and his desire to help to promote it.

"He has an impeccable technique and is an authentic ambassador of flamenco music throughout the whole world" José Manuel Gamboa

"A giant of the flamenco tradition" The Times

"He has a terrifyingly good technique and an absolute dominance of the guitar, filling the concert hall with crystalline clarity" El Mundo

Sobre el compositor

Juan Martín aprendió su arte en la tierra de su origen, Andalucía, en el sur de España, donde pasó sus primeros años de formación y donde aún conserva una casa. De adolescente tocó en fiestas locales, bodas y bautizos, desarrollando su conocimiento y habilidades en las disciplinas de las tradiciones más puras del flamenco. A los 17 años, ya tocando profesionalmente, actuó en la película *Donde tu estés*, rodada en la región de Málaga, y a los 18 años se fue a Madrid, donde adquirió una amplia experiencia con muchos cantaores, guitarristas y bailaores destacados. Fue influenciado en gran medida por el ejemplo y el estímulo del legendario guitarrista Niño Ricardo y Juan era un visitante habitual en la casa de Paco de Lucía en Madrid.

Estos primeros años tocando en el corazón del flamenco proporcionaron la base para su carrera posterior como solista y líder de sus propias compañías de baile, una vocación desafiante que le ha traído la aclamación internacional como un innovador intérprete de concierto, locutor y artista de grabación.

Durante dos años consecutivos fue votado como ganador de la revista norteamericana *Guitar Player* en la sección de flamenco, y fue invitado a actuar en la celebración del 90 cumpleaños de Picasso. Ha actuado en los principales festivales de arte, incluido el Festival de Jazz de Montreux con Miles Davis y Herbie Hancock, el Primer Congreso Mundial de Guitarra en los Estados Unidos, Estambul, Hong Kong, Shanghai y The London Guitar Summit. En Andalucía participó en festivales de flamenco en las provincias de Ojén, Málaga y Cádiz, compartiendo cartel con Paco Cepero, Paco del Gastor, Vicente Amigo, El Pele, El Cabrero, Juanito Villar, La Macanita y Parilla de Jerez, Amparo Heredia 'La Repompilla' y David Morales, el bailaor Linense.

Su interés por las raíces árabes del flamenco lo llevó a grabar *Música Alhambra* redescubriendo la música andalusí y sefardí de los siglos XII y XIII. "Martín abarca los siglos con una mezcla de lo deslumbrante y lo profundo", comentó el periódico británico *The Observer*. Los CD más recientes han incluido *La Guitarra – Mi Vida* (2015) con Chaparro de Málaga, *Guitar Maestro*, una colección de sus grabaciones que incluyen piezas con la Royal Philharmonic Orchestra de su álbum *Serenade*, *Los Primeros Años*, piezas grabadas con sellos discográficos importantes como Decca, EMI y con el cante de Rafael Romero 'El Gallina', *El Alquimista* grabado en Andalucía, *Riquezas* con el cantaor flamenco San Roqueño, Antonio Aparecida, el *Camino Latino* con influencia latina con Airto Moreira y Flora Purim, *Live en Directo*, una grabación en vivo de 2 CD de una actuación en el Barbican de Londres de su compañía de baile y una Divucsa recopilación de 3 CD *El Embrujo de la Guitarra* con composiciones suyas entre otros guitarristas como Paco de Lucía y Manolo Sanlúcar.

Éstas y sus otras muchas grabaciones están disponibles en todos los principales servicios de descarga y transmisión. Sus giras alrededor del mundo han incluido China, Australia, Irán, Estados Unidos, Canadá y Europa y 22 conciertos en el Reino Unido con la bailaora española numero uno, Eva La Yerbabuena.

Sus composiciones reúnen una destilación de su amplio conocimiento de lo tradicional, estilos flamencos con sus propias interpretaciones inventivas de la música. Muestran su dominio de la amplia gama de palos flamencos (formas rítmicas) que se originan en las diferentes regiones de Andalucía y su distintivo sello propio y espíritu de flamenco puro, a menudo iluminado por un fuerte sentido visual de los lugares, personas y pinturas, que caracterizan la notable variedad y profundidad de su arte actual. Especialmente característico de su forma de tocar es una sensibilidad inusualmente profunda a las bellezas del sonido de las que es capaz su guitarra y un ímpetu rítmico poderoso.

Éstas cualidades le han traido invitaciones para ofrecer recitales como guitarra solista en algunas de las mejores salas de conciertos del mundo, desde los salones Wigmore y Queen Elizabeth de Londres hasta el Herbst de San Francisco, las salas Carnegie y Merkin de Nueva York, el Tonhalle de Zúrich, Alte Oper de Frankfurt, Concertgebouw de Amsterdam, el Conservatorio de Sydney, City Hall de Hong Kong hasta la Casa de Pilatos, Sevilla. Los críticos han comparado sus composiciones con las de los grandes compositores españoles, Tárrega y Turina.

Un deseo apasionado de comunicar los misterios del flamenco a una audiencia más amplia de guitarristas llevó a la publicación en 1978 del Método de Guitarra de Juan Martín, *El Arte Flamenco de la Guitarra*, con CD. Su serie de videos de 1991, *La Guitarra Flamenca*, ahora es relanzada por Faber como un libro con 2 DVD. Mel Bay publica dos volúmenes de solos graduados progresivamente, cada uno con video y audio en línea, *Solos Flamencos*, así como otros dos libros con videos en línea *Essential Flamenco*, que se han convertido en best sellers.

Desde 2011 lleva a cabo un curso anual de guitarra en Ronda, Andalucía y esto, junto con su exigente agenda, enfatiza la profunda lealtad de Juan a las raíces de su arte y su deseo de ayudar a fomentarlo.

"Tiene una técnica impecable y es un auténtico embajador de la música flamenca en todo el mundo"
José Manuel Gamboa

"Un coloso de la tradición flamenca" The Times, Londres

"Tiene una técnica terriblemente buena y un dominio absoluto de la guitarra, llenando la sala de conciertos con claridad cristalina" El Mundo

JUAN MARTÍN PUBLICATIONS/PUBLICACIONES

GUITAR MUSIC BOOKS BY JUAN MARTÍN with Patrick Campbell.

All transcriptions in guitar tablature (cifra) and staff notation

JUAN MARTÍN'S GUITAR METHOD: EL ARTE FLAMENCO DE LA GUITARRA (2nd Edition 2017) with 60 minute CD, United Music Publishing UK

ANDALUCIAN SUITE NO.1 – 4 guitar solos from the album 'The Andalucian Suites' (FV01), Mel Bay Publications, Inc. USA

THE EXCITING SOUND OF FLAMENCO, Volumes 1 and 2, each with 2 solos from 'The Early Years' (FV14). United Music Publishing UK

GUITAR MUSIC BOOKS WITH DVDS BY JUAN MARTÍN with Patrick Campbell

ESSENTIAL FLAMENCO GUITAR Vol. 1 and 2 An in-depth course for absolute beginners to more advanced players with online video, Mel Bay Publications, Inc. USA

PLAY FLAMENCO GUITAR WITH JUAN MARTÍN: SOLOS FLAMENCOS. Vol. 1 and 2 Grades 0-5 and 6-8, each with online video and audio, Mel Bay Publications, Inc. USA

LA GUITARRA FLAMENCA: Complete method book with 2 DVDs, Faber Music, UK

DVDS OF JUAN MARTÍN'S FLAMENCO DANCE COMPANY

1992 **JUAN MARTÍN AND HIS FLAMENCO DANCE COMPANY FROM SEVILLE** available online
2009 **LIVE AT THE ROMAN AMPHITHEATRE, ISTANBUL**, Mel Bay Publications, Inc. USA
2010 **LIVE IN LONDON AT THE BARBICAN** (VFV14)

FLAMENCOVISION ALBUMS RECORDED BY JUAN MARTÍN: CDs, downloads and streaming, most recent first:

2019 **GUITAR MAESTRO, THE JUAN MARTÍN COLLECTION** (4 CD compilation) FV17
2018 **PAINTER IN SOUND**, with Mark Isham (FV16)
2015 **LA GUITARRA – MI VIDA**, duos with Chaparro de Málaga (FV15)
2014 **THE EARLY YEARS, LOS PRIMEROS AÑOS**, early recordings and tracks with singer Rafael Romero (FV14)
2008 **SOLO** (FV012)
2008 **SERENADE, WITH THE ROYAL PHILHARMONIC ORCHESTRA** (FV11)
2006 **RUMBAS ORIGINALES**, a collection of rumba compositions (FV10)
2003 **LIVE EN DIRECTO**, a double CD of Juan Martín's dance company live at the Barbican (FV09)
2002 **CAMINO LATINO**, the latin influence on flamenco (FV08)
2002 **RIQUEZAS**, with singer Antonio Aparecida (FV07)
2000 **EL ALQUIMISTA**, The Alchemist (FV06)
1998 **ARTE FLAMENCO PURO**, with Juan Martín's dance group (FV05)
1996 **MUSICA ALHAMBRA**, with Abdul Salam Kheir (oud) and others, (FV04)
1994 **PICASSO PORTRAITS**, with Juan Martín's fusion group (FV03)
1993 **LUNA NEGRA** (FV02)
1990 **THE ANDALUCIAN SUITES**, (FV01) also Edición española: Divucsa

EARLY MAJOR RELEASES BY JUAN MARTÍN

1974 **THE EXCITING SOUND OF FLAMENCO,** ARGO
1976 **THE FLAMENCO SOUL OF JUAN MARTÍN,** DECCA
1977 **OLÉ DON JUAN, FLAMENCO EN ANDALUCÍA,** EMI
1978 **ROMANCE,** EMI
1981 **PICASSO PORTRAITS,** POLYDOR
1984 **SERENADE,** WEA
1985 **SOLO,** WEA
1986 **PAINTER IN SOUND,** WEA/BMG
1988 **THROUGH THE MOVING WINDOW,** BMG

All products available from **www.flamencovision.com**

Todos estos productos de Flamencovision, más los libros y DVDs, se puede conseguir de **www.flamencovision.com**

MEL BAY ®